THE COMMONWEALTH AND INTERNATIONAL LIBRARY

Joint Chairmen of the Honorary Editorial Advisory Board

SIR ROBERT ROBINSON, O.M., F.R.S. LONDON

DEAN ATHELSTAN SPILHAUS, MINNESOTA

SOCIAL WORK DIVISION

General Editor: JEAN P. NURSTEN

Communication in Social Work

BY
PETER R. DAY
Tutor, Department of Adult Education
University of Nottingham

PERGAMON PRESS
OXFORD · NEW YORK · TORONTO
SYDNEY . BRAUNSCHWEIG

Pergamon Press Ltd., Headington Hill Hall, Oxford

Pergamon Press Inc., Maxwell House, Fairview Park, Elmsford, New York 10523

Pergamon of Canada Ltd., 207 Queen's Quay West, Toronto 1

Pergamon Press (Aust.) Pty. Ltd., 19a Boundary Street, Rushcutters Bay, N.S.W. 2011, Australia

Vieweg & Sohn GmbH, Burgplatz 1, Braunschweig

First edition 1972

Library of Congress Cataloging in Publication Data

Day, Peter Russell, 1933–
    Communication in social work.

    (Commonwealth and international library. Social work division).
    Bibliography: p.
    1. Social service. 2. Communication—Social aspects. I. Title.
HV41.D27   361   72–8466
ISBN 0–08–017064–1
ISBN 0–08–017065–X (pbk.)

Printed in Great Britain by A. Brown & Sons, Limited, Hull.

ISBN 0 08 017064 1 (hard cover)
ISBN 0 08 017065 X (flexicover)

Preface

THE diagram entitled Processes of Communication in Chapter 1 is from *Communication* by Colin Mares (page 44). I am obliged to the English Universities Press Ltd., for permission to reproduce it. I am obliged to Mr. Hunter Diack for permission to use his diagram entitled Dynamics of Communication. This is also in Chapter 1 and is from his book *Language for Teaching* (page 112), published by Chatto and Windus. I am grateful to my father, Mr. Leslie Day, for his help in preparing reproductions of these diagrams for this book. I thank Mrs. Sheila Allard, Miss Jenny Begg and Mrs. Jessie Hill, for their patient work in preparing drafts of the manuscript.

An attempt to make further specific acknowledgements to other people who have helped me might be invidious. For one thing, many of them cannot be named for professional reasons. But I wish to record my gratitude to those people, clients, social workers, teachers, students and others who have given me stimulation and help.

PETER R. DAY

We are all subtle interpreters of social signals. But we like to limit the number of readings and adjustments we make. This is a pity since, if we looked more closely, we might be surprised by how much we had to re-interpret some of our pictures of society.

RICHARD HOGGART
(BBC Reith Lectures 1971)

We all must continually learn to unlearn much we have learned and learn to learn much that we have not been taught. Only thus do we and our subject grow.

R. D. LAING
(Intervention in Social Situations. A.F.C.W.
and Philadelphia Association Ltd. 1969)

Contents

Preface   vii

1. The Nature of Communication   1

2. Communication Processes in Social Work   17

3. Some Influences on Communication between Client and
    Social Worker   31

4. Social Factors in Communication   43

5. Communication and the Helping Process   59

6. The Social Agency and the Social Worker   77

7. The Community, the Social Agency and the Social
    Worker   91

Notes   107

Bibliography   111

Index   117

CHAPTER 1

The Nature of Communication

1. *Living and communicating*

For nearly thirty years we have lived with the risk of nuclear holocaust. We may read and hear a great deal about other very serious problems of our human and non-human environment which affect our chances of survival. As far as our existing knowledge goes we are not particularly well equipped to cope with environmental pollution, depletion of resources and overpopulation. Sometimes people, and often politicians, behave as though industrial growth and consumption can go on expanding forever. They overlook, it seems, a growing appreciation of the fearful crises which technical advances can cause.

Meyer (1970) in *Social Work Practice* has discussed the critical problems produced by urban industrial society. Increasing numbers of people live in urban areas. The number of cities will increase and existing ones will get bigger. Growth leads to serious physical problems. We have considerable evidence that animals show signs of increased stress in overcrowded conditions. In human beings overcrowding might account for increased delinquency. Increasing crime rates and the trends in urbanisation are moving in the same direction (McClintock and Avison, 1968). It has been suggested that overcrowding might account for other contemporary urban phenomena such as withdrawal or alienation from society (hippies and revolutionaries, for example), sexual promiscuity and political apathy (Timms, 1969). Some of our problems of squalid neighbourhoods, overcrowding and misery could be solved given the necessary resources and the capacity for using them systematically. Meyer discusses some of the psychological and

1

community problems of urban areas. People need a sense of community and identity. Such needs are hard to describe. But by upsetting traditional social structures such as the family and the neighbourhood, habitual ways of life and relationships between people are disturbed. The hierarchical structure of roles in industrial society distributes power and authority unequally and as unacceptably as in previous status structures. In a large urban area a person can feel an emptiness, a feeling of being lost or of not belonging. But to achieve a sense of identity a person needs to feel that he has a place or a position in a community. A pluralist society also involves potential or actual conflicts of loyalty. A man's place in society is often not simple. He belongs to many groups whose demands are not always compatible. They have their own sets of values. Side by side with technical advances, such as new methods of communication, there is evidence, not of greater co-operation, but rather of increasing loneliness, isolation or hostility. As interaction between groups increases they often seem to become more violently opposed to one another. Pressures and tensions are generated which increasingly disrupt community life. People ask how the growth of urban problems is to be controlled and how are relationships between people to be organised? How can systems of communication and control be devised so as to reconcile the multiplicity of competing interests and thus reduce alienation or impoverishment? The inability to cope satisfactorily with such problems is sometimes due to changes in moral standards. Failures of communication are serious when we are unable to make distinctions between situations in which we act and to decide how we want to control various kinds of relationships. These failures may arise out of the communication process itself: we may be unable to share ways of analysing criteria or norms as guides to action.

Williams (1968) has commented on attitudes towards the growth of modern communications. Many people have seen this not as an expansion of men's powers to learn and to exchange ideas and experiences, but as a new method of government or a new opportunity for trade. All the new means of communication have been abused for political control (as in propaganda) or for commercial profit (as in advertising). We can protest against such uses but unless we have a clear alternative version of human society we are not likely to make our protests effective.

Williams points out an important danger in discussions of communication. Many people seem to assume that first there is reality and then communication about it. In his view the commonest political error is the assumption that power is the reality of the whole social process, and so the only context of politics. He points out that trade and production are often taken for granted, requiring no justification or scrutiny. But the business of society cannot be confined to these ends: the struggle to learn, to educate, describe and understand is a central part of being human. This struggle is not begun at second hand after reality has occurred. In itself it is a major way in which reality is continually formed and changed. "Society" is a process of learning and communication and not only a political and economic pattern.

Later in this book I will try to develop some of the notions which have been introduced here. The immediate purpose has been to attempt to justify the study of the communication process. Briefly the argument is that such a study may contribute to our ways of dealing with serious problems of the environment and human relations. At present we are poorly equipped to deal with them although there is a growing sense of urgency. If we are to survive, and how we are to do this, depends on making considerable changes in human behaviour. In the past people could satisfactorily communicate largely within their own small groups. The growing complexity of society and new kinds of social problems lead to a need for new methods of communication. In themselves, they do not provide a panacea: increased communication can lead to intensification of conflict. Some new patterns of communication evolve spontaneously while others are introduced deliberately. Adequate communication can be an important factor in close co-operation, in reducing alienation, and in building understanding between groups of people and between individuals. We need to consider and to study in detail the variety of ways in which we communicate and the media which we use. This may help us towards a better understanding of human behaviour and in paying attention to building communities in which people will be able to lead satisfactory lives.

2. *The study of communication*

At the outset we have to recognise certain difficulties quite clearly. The various aspects of communication as they are studied in different disciplines do not form a unified field of study. According to Cherry (1961) the understanding of the whole communication process is at present an unattainable ideal. But this book attempts to discuss social work from the point of view of communication theories and research in the belief that this is a useful way to approach the study of helping processes. It is assumed that further study of the subject will be of help to social workers in serving their clients. Communication concepts are relevant to casework and group and community work. In any case it is difficult to make rigid distinctions between the methods of social work practice. One of the many dangers in trying to communicate about communication, and to some extent about social work, is that of viewing the subject in such wide terms that statements about it become vague and imprecise. On the other hand, undue concern or selfconsciousness in attempting to use a means of communication, such as written language, may lead to a kind of semi-paralysis. Such fears about the attempt to communicate may lead to failure to make statements or assert opinions. The pitfalls are great.

The main themes of the book are outlined in this chapter and I attempt to clarify some of the concepts which will be employed in later chapters. This chapter is therefore concerned with the elements of the communication process and their dynamic interaction. It concludes by linking these to social work and with a plan of the rest of the book. Communication is any transmission of information by means of (a) the sending, (b) the conduction, and (c) the reception of (d) a message (Aranguren, 1967). It means a sharing of elements of behaviour or modes of life by the existence of sets of rules. It is essentially the relationship set up by the transmission of stimuli and the evocation of responses (Cherry, 1961). The meaning of a communication is present in the sending and receiving stages but not in the transmission stage. Words mean nothing in themselves. They are tools to convey meaning.

The study of human communication can be subdivided into three areas which are interdependent. Syntactics is concerned with the problems of transmitting information, the problems of coding, channels and their capacity, noise, redundancy and other statistical properties of language. Information theory is a mathematical technique for measuring the effectiveness of sign transmission in a man-made system. What is measured is the speed or economy with which sign information (uncertainty reduction) can be brought about. Semantics is mainly concerned with the problem of verbal meaning, whereas syntactics is concerned with the arrangement of words and the construction of sentences. The third area is Pragmatics which is concerned with the effect of communication on behaviour. This area is the concern of this book. Pragmatics is concerned with the meanings of words and also with their non-verbal concomitants and the language of gestures and body movements. All behaviour may be communicative and there are often communicational clues in the context in which behaviour occurs. From this point of view all communication affects behaviour (Watzlawick *et al.*, 1968). Communication generally refers to the organisation, transmission and reception of messages. It is not equivalent to interaction which is a term of wider scope.

Communication as Williams has remarked (see above) may be used to increase conflict and competitiveness between people. Sharing a language with other people provides a subtle and powerful tool for controlling the behaviour of others, for stirring up rivalries, advancing one's own goals and for exploiting other people. Communication is a social activity. The evolution of various systems of communications have made social life possible. Language permits the organisation of thought. This leads to self-awareness and social responsibility, seen in the development of legal and moral systems.

Communication necessarily entails organisation and structure. Social interaction, of course, does not depend entirely on verbal language. Non-verbal communications, such as nods, smiles, frowns, gestures and other physical movements, also convey understanding and response, and form systems of communication in themselves or are part of other systems (Cherry, 1961).

Communication is thus a basic tool of interpersonal relationships and is simultaneously (a) for gathering information and (b) for potential influence by all members of the relationship. A communication not only conveys information but at the same time imposes behaviour. These two operations are known as the "report" and the "command" aspects of any communication (Watzlawick *et al.*, 1968). The idea of social networks is helpful when one is studying structural aspects of groups of people. Some definite kinds of group structure are often discussed—such as dictatorships or collaborative groups. Ideas about group structures can be oversimplified and networks of communication in groups in reality are often complex. However, the term network is a useful one to describe sets of social relationships between people, some of whom are directly in touch with each other, some of whom are indirectly in touch with others (i.e. through a third party), and some of whom are not in touch with anyone else. Because of the range of possible relationships a single person may have, it is often necessary to think in terms of networks in the plural, and of networks which overlap with each other.

Thinking of networks of interpersonal relationships leads to consideration of interaction as a system. A system can be defined as a set of objects with relationships between the objects and between their attributes. It is a whole which is compounded of many parts. Attributes of things or people are properties which are assumed by the observer to be significant (Cherry, 1961). A system is a collection of components or devices intended to perform some specified function or functions. Human societies have evolved over long periods of time and have developed a capacity of responding to a wide range of situations. In this they differ from other kinds of systems, such as machines used in engineering, or computers. The science of cybernetics is concerned with control and communication processes in machines and animals, and it has influenced thinking about learning, thought processes and purposeful behaviour in animals and human beings. Cybernetic models may be of help in studying human groups. Each individual may be conceived as an information processing system. All information processes attributed to a group are actually performed by individuals as members of a group. For present purposes we need not pursue this topic in detail but some implications are important in studying human communication processes. We have seen that the term system implies interrelated parts that function in relation to each other. In human systems people are in contact with and affect and are affected by others. The family operates in relation to other families and groups in society. In studying communication processes, networks, and systems it is important to look at their interdependent components and the relationships between different networks and systems.

Maier (1965) has discussed the systems formed by the social networks of client and helper and the influences on them. Four different "helping systems" may be distinguished.

1. The "individual system". This involves a one to one relationship between the client and the helper.
2. The "system of the group". The family or another appropriate group could be selected as the most advisable system within which the helping process is applied. The individual is helped within the group which includes the helper.
3. The "auxiliary system". Parents, teachers or employers, for example, may be selected as those with whom the helper will deal.
4. Important services or policies directly affecting the individual's life are brought to the foreground, and the helping process seeks to achieve the application, or a change in the application, of services in a way which would help the individual.

Communication failure is often attributed to the ambiguities and deficiencies of the medium used, language for example, as if language is constructed to mislead the people who use it. But words are instruments of expression and thought and can be used well or badly according to the perception, motivation and capacity of the people who use them. If faulty transmission occurs it is important to look at other human limitations in the first place, rather than the deficiencies of language. Language is a vocabulary and a way of using it. A sign is a mark used conventionally to denote something other than itself. It is therefore something which has to be interpreted. It may be misunderstood. In the case of linguistic signs, taking the form of a code, it may be unintelligible to anyone who does not possess the key. A sign does not, of itself, transmit any message. It must be deciphered. Signs may refer to the past but their meaning relates to the future. Footprints are an example. Human actions are determined by anticipation based on signs of the past, on present attitudes, or on signals referring directly to the future. Thinking of signs in this way emphasises the fact that the information they give always refers to the future and is therefore predictive. A sign has anticipatory value making it possible to get ahead of events and avoid or modify them.

Two aspects of language need to be distinguished: (a) the descriptive or cognitive and (b) the emotive. This distinction is between (a) the functions of language as representation and (b) its function of modifying or provoking behaviour. Language helps in the formation of concepts. Concepts abstract the essence of things and facilitate classification of objects and events. They are formed through experience of reality, and one of the most important elements in concept formation is thus the process of perception. The response of any person to some sign or stimulus will depend on the individual's past experience and present state. Every individual has different past experiences. Psychological set is a temporary condition of an organism which facilitates a certain more or less specific type of activity or response. It influences the individual's formation of associations, and brings to bear certain determining tendencies and thus influences his mode of response, his perceptions and his recognition of signs. Set depends on past experience and on a person's predictions or anticipations about the likely consequences of his actions or responses.

3. *Processes of communication*

The accompanying diagram (taken from Mares, 1966) is helpful in analysing the processes of communication. It shows how different aspects of communication are interrelated and that transmission and reception are not entirely separate processes. Communication is seen as a complex process of interaction between thought, language, and action. Whenever one person communicates with another he communicates something through a particular medium and for a particular purpose. Messages set up a relationship between transmitter and receiver. Communication is a two-way affair and feedback plays an important part in affecting subsequent communication. Noise may affect the whole process or different parts of the process. When one person speaks to another three components are essential. A coding and decoding device is required to translate ideas into messages and messages into ideas. A transmitting mechanism is necessary to send out the signals in which the message is encoded. A receiving mechanism is necessary to pick up the signals which are then decoded into messages. Information has to be sorted or organised either for transmission or assimilation. This process is an aspect of thinking. In speaking (or gesturing) information is transmitted. Then the information is received.

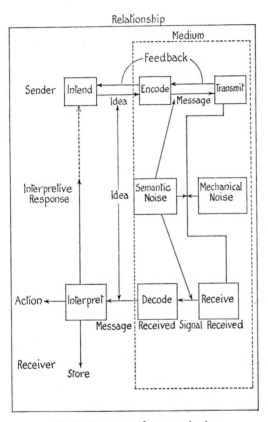

Fig. 1. Processes of communication.

The diagram shows various kinds of behaviour that are present when one person speaks to another. The sender's intentions include all the behaviour which occurs before the message is put into words. This emphasises the purposive nature of communication. When the sender of a message decides to communicate information to someone else he encodes the information in a form in which it may be transmitted. If different media are available, he chooses the medium of communication. A medium is any instrument for transmitting information whether this is a human sense or combination of senses or a natural or man made vehicle of transmission. Every vehicle is selective in terms of the material it transmits. His choice of medium will be determined by a number of factors such as the nature of the information, the people to whom he is transmitting, the situation at the time, and the responses he anticipates. The sender works out what he has to say, to whom he wishes to say it, and tries to find out how best to ensure that the people who should receive the message do receive it. In decoding the message the receiver discriminates (a) between the actual elements of the message and any noise which may be present, and (b) the interaction of these elements with previous perceptions. Interpretation refers to the response to the message when it is decoded. Symbols are translated into ideas. When the ideas are understood they influence further behaviour. They have to be fitted in to the receiver's previous experience and they then act as a stimulus for further communication or other action. Decision and subsequent action derive directly from interpretation. A possible action may be to store the information. Noise is any undesired disturbance in a communication system. Mechanical noise may be (a) outside interference which affects the physical clarity of the signal, (b) interference arising from faults in the transmitting and receiving mechanisms themselves. Semantic noise refers to any kind of alteration which is made to the message as sent, by the fallibility of the medium, e.g. language. The same word can mean different things to different people. When B interprets a word used by A in a way which differs from A's intended meaning this is semantic noise.

Thinking of the elements of a communication system suggests possible sources of failures or breakdowns in communication. It is often difficult to disentangle them and our ideas about communication systems are sometimes ambiguous. Seven categories are useful in describing a system, however. A simple communication model consists of a sender, a receiver, a message, a channel, a means of encoding and decoding messages, and a feedback system. Discussing this model Timms (1962) pointed out that it is difficult in practice to identify the person who initiates a communication but theoretically it is necessary to begin with someone who wants to affect someone else, to get something across with a view to achieving a particular objective.

4. *Dynamics of communication*

The diagram illustrating the dynamics of communication is taken from Diack (1966). Person A wishes to convey information to B. Before he speaks he has certain ideas in his mind to which he wishes B to respond; he may hope that B will act in certain ways on what he conveys. What

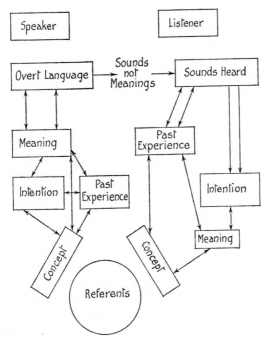

Fig. 2. Dynamics of communication.

A says to B will depend on the situation, on A's previous experience of similar situations, and his previous experience, if any, of talking to B. A talks to B about something. He uses words—symbols which stand for something. The meaning of the words to B will depend on the situation in which they are spoken. A may intend to convey a double or hidden meaning. A's message may not correspond with other aspects of A's behaviour. A's tone of voice may imply that the opposite of what he actually says is intended. The message may be interpreted by B in a way opposite to that intended by A.

B's response to what A says will depend on the unique situation in which the conversation takes place and on B's expectation of A in the situation before he speaks. B may have had some ideas about what A might say or do in the situation beforehand and what A says may confirm (or not confirm) these ideas. What A says will be weighed by B in the light of the whole situation, B's past experience of similar situations and B's previous experience of A. For example, if B fears A, or if B is not paying attention to what A says, such factors, regarded as psychological noise, might interfere with B's reception of the message. B may not understand the words A uses in the same way as A understands them. Their speech habits may differ and their uses of language may not be identical.

Communication between A and B is thus subject to a number of uncertainties. A's and B's concepts of what they are talking about may differ. Their purposes and intentions affect both what they say and how they say it. The listener usually has a different starting point from the speaker. At first he may not have a purpose in listening. As soon as he has a purpose he becomes involved in the process of putting meanings into the words he hears (and the other communicative acts of the speaker) by reference to his past experience and the present context. Redundancy is the inclusion in a message of unnecessary and therefore non-informative items. Given a certain letter or word or a sequence of letters or words the next unit in a message is to a large degree statistically determined. Redundancy thus occurs when words add nothing to meaning already obtained. Condensation is the opposite of redundancy and refers to the packing of distinct meanings into a single image. As Freud showed, this is a common dream mechanism. Information is a term which covers any kind of message which is transmissible from sender to receiver. Feedback is the term used for the return of impulses to a control centre where they play a part in further control, as in the case of impulses produced by muscular activity returning to the brain, informing it of the posture of the muscles and thus contributing to further control of these muscles. In a sense it is comparable with the functions of a governor on a steam engine which feeds back the information that more or less steam is needed.

Leavitt and Muller (1951) carried out an experiment to see how far the transmission of information from person A to person B was influenced by the return of information from B to A. They showed statistically that the accuracy of information conveyed increased steadily in conditions ranging from "zero feedback" to "free feedback". Increased accuracy due to emotional feedback lessened feelings of frustration between experimenter and subject. Frustration had created hostility between them and this was reduced as each understood the other more clearly. More efficient communication thus effectively increased the feeling of achievement and security in their relationship. Problem solving behaviour may be described in terms of feedback. Trial and error may be used where the method of solution of the problem is not clear, that is, in a difficult problem. In each case of error, information about lack of success of the trial is fed back to influence further activity. Success in solving a problem stops any further modification of the trial and error activity; equilibrium has been reached.

Thinking or reasoning is essentially what occurs in experience when an organism (human or animal) meets, recognises and solves a problem. Problem solving is implicit in thinking. In explicit problem solving the test of a guess is by reference to experience. In thought (implicit problem solving) the test is by reference to implicit experience. The test tells us that a trial has been a success or a failure, that the problem has been solved or not solved. As in overt problem solving in thinking there is a continuous feedback of information regarding the failure of successive trial answers or guesses. This feedback keeps the thought process going, regulating mental activity and maintaining tension. From this point of view thinking may be regarded as an adaptive activity, helping to maintain equilibrium (or homeostasis), and as a process continuous with learning and problem solving. To the extent that problems are solved by trial and error, thought processes also progress by trial and error. In the common-sense use of the term problem solving goes together with thought. A thought process may be regarded as a process of solving a problem in a manner which makes the attempts, the trials, errors and the successful solution hidden from direct observation (Sluckin, 1960).

The situation in which communication occurs affects the content of communication. Physical and psychological noise may interfere with transmission and reception. Where more than two people are involved, communication may be mediated through other people whether they are present or not. This adds further dimensions to the process. In studying groups or organisations it is important to know whether A may speak directly to B or only through C or D, or how in fact A and B do communicate with each other or with other people. It is also important to know whether communication is in one direction only, or whether B is able to reply to A.

5. *Social work*

Social casework has been defined as a personal service for individuals who require skilled help in resolving some personal or family problem. Its aim is to relieve stress, both material and emotional, and to help the client to achieve his maximum well being. The caseworker seeks to do this by means of a careful study of the client in his family and social setting and of his problem, by the establishment of a co-operative relationship with him in which his own capacity for dealing with his problem is increased, and by the mobilisation of such other resources or professional aid as may be appropriate (Davison, 1965).

The processes mentioned in this definition involve the transmission, reception and interpretation of non-verbal and verbal messages in order to communicate the nature of experience by sharing thought and feeling and in order to influence the behaviour of others. They also involve other activities which may occur as the result of communication. Skill in receiving, understanding and sending non-verbal and verbal communications may be regarded as being of great importance in the interaction between the social worker and the person or family seeking, or thought to need his help. It is part of the social worker's function to mobilise other resources or professional aid which may be appropriate in meeting clients' needs. The social worker thus has to be able to draw on the resources of his own or other organisations in helping the client. The social worker has an interest in the development of the services within which, or in association with which, he works. Because of his direct contact with the people his agency serves he can often provide information about the extent to which it is providing the service it was set up to provide and about areas of unmet need. Potentially there is much that the social worker can contribute in the alteration or formulation of social policy. The social worker's capacity to communicate within his organisation and other groups in the community is thus of great importance as an influence in social affairs (Donnison *et al.*, 1965).

Some of the points made theoretically in this chapter about communication processes in social work are developed in Chapter 2. Chapter 3 is concerned with some influences on communication between client and social worker and Chapter 4 with social factors in communication. Work on communication and learning and their role in the helping process is considered in Chapter 5. Chapter 6 reviews communication in social agencies. Chapter 7 considers communication and its role in interagency co-ordination and in other groups in the community. The theoretical and research work discussed in the two final chapters is applicable to other groups as well as to social agencies, although the illustrations which form the basis for discussion are of communication processes in these settings.

CHAPTER 2

Communication Processes in Social Work

1. Social-work help: information, advice and material aid

People who require help with personal and social problems go to social agencies in a variety of ways. They may go on their own initiative or they may be referred by someone else. They may accept referral willingly, or they may resent being referred. There will be variations in their knowledge of the functions of the social services. Some people may have been given information about an agency by a friend or by the person referring them, while others may know very little about the service provided. The single word "client" is commonly used to denote the person who requires the services of a social agency. Some social workers dislike the use of this word because they dislike its connotations, but it will be used here in the absence of more satisfactory alternatives.

The range of needs presented to social agencies is wide. In common with many other organisations available to the public they receive requests for straightforward information, for example, about services available, or eligibility for financial or material help, opportunities for voluntary service, or the possibility of paid employment in the social services. In situations of this kind the receptionist or the social worker may be able to provide clear information which meets an inquirer's needs. A single, brief, conversation may be all that is necessary. It should not be assumed, however, that the giving of information is always a simple matter. Very often, of course, simple and straightforward answers to questions about applying for sickness benefit, or where to find out about renting a council house, are all that is necessary. But to give such information acceptably is an important part of an agency's public

17

relations task. The reception of members of the public and their courteous treatment are important ways in which the staff of a social agency convey their attitudes towards their clients.

Information and advice can be given in ways which enable clients to ask further questions if necessary, or to seek further help. An initial inquiry may turn out to be less simple than it at first appeared. A brusque, uninterested, perfunctory response to a client may discourage him from asking for help which he requires. A first question may not be what a questioner mainly wants to know. In a strange situation a person may feel his way gradually, not stating immediately what it is he wants to ask about, but waiting until he senses whether he is likely to get a sympathetic, or at least a courteous response. There are other reasons why the client who makes an inquiry should be allowed to take a reasonable amount of time and encouraged to ask further questions if necessary. Many people find it difficult to absorb information quickly, especially if this involves understanding rules and regulations or official forms or documents. Supplementary explanations are often necessary. A person who feels unsure of himself may find it difficult to say that he does not understand when in fact he is unable to interpret a form or a verbal explanation. The interviewer needs to ascertain too that he has understood the inquiry as well as that the client understands the answer.

Another kind of service which may be needed is material help. Examples are residential care either for a child or an adult, an appliance to aid a physically handicapped person, domestic assistance in the house, or other forms of physical or financial help.

Requests for information, advice, or material help sometimes reveal situations which are complicated and in which additional help is needed. For example, sometimes giving advice is futile if the client is unable to act on it. A distinction is sometimes usefully made between the "presenting request or problem" and associated or underlying problems. If, in the initial interview, the social worker is able to help the client to relax, and to give his account of why he has come in his own words, this gives the social worker the opportunity to try to assess the situation, and to decide as soon as possible, whether the client's request comes within the scope of the agency. Unnecessary questioning, which can be annoying, can thus be avoided. At the same time, the social worker needs to have sufficient information on which to base a valid judgment. A failure to ask questions can mean that the social worker fails to grasp the essentials of the situation. It can also indicate carelessness or lack of interest.

The case summary which follows is a brief account of some interviews between a medical social worker and one of her clients. It is an illustration of a situation where information and advice on their own would not have been helpful to the client. It illustrates some of the points which have been made so far and leads to further discussion of aspects of communication in the helping process.

2. *Mr. Clark: Summary*

Mr. Clark, aged 69, was admitted to hospital following a coronary thrombosis. He made a partial recovery, and his doctor thought that he might be able to manage at home with domestic help because he lived alone. It was likely that before long some form of residential care would be necessary. The doctor advised Mr. Clark to think about this possibility, and asked the Medical Social Worker to see him before he left hospital.

Miss Smith, the medical social worker, discussed the possibility of admission to a home with Mr. Clark, who said he would think about it. He would not accept a home help. Miss Smith noted that Mr. Clark seemed to take pride in his independence. She visited him one month after he left hospital. He said that his doctor had strongly advised him to rest as much as possible, but he could not accept this advice because he could not tolerate an untidy or dirty home. He seemed to be worried about his situation but fearful of changing his way of life. He agreed to Miss Smith contacting the Meals on Wheels Service. She arranged this after her visit and wrote informing him of it.

Three weeks later Miss Smith visited Mr. Clark again. His doctor had again advised him to rest but he felt, as he had told her before, that this advice was difficult to follow. He was still considering entering a home but feared losing his freedom. After this visit Miss Smith made inquiries about vacancies in Homes and after three weeks visited Mr.

Clark again. They discussed the results of the inquiries she had made but Mr. Clark was still feeling very mixed about what he should do.

Miss Smith continued to make inquiries and discovered a private home which Mr. Clark might be able to enter and to which he could take his furniture and other possessions. On her next visit she found that Mr. Clark had had another slight heart attack and the doctor has asked him how much longer he thought he could continue to live alone. They discussed the private home, the financial arrangements and method of application. Mr. Clark asked Miss Smith a great deal about the home and then he seemed suddenly to make up his mind. He decided to go to see the warden of the Home the following day.

After Mr. Clark's visit the warden of the home telephoned Miss Smith. Mr. Clark had filled in an application form and was now on the waiting list. Miss Smith continued to visit her client while he was waiting for a vacancy.

3. *Social-work help: emotional support in adapting to change*

Giving Mr. Clark information or advice alone would not have helped him sufficiently. He was usually able to cope with his affairs without help but found it difficult to resolve the problems associated with his illness and his feelings about entering a home. The medical social worker assisted him by providing the emotional support which he needed and by helping him to think about his situation through discussion of alternative courses of action. It was only when the social worker had helped Mr. Clark come to terms with his anxieties that he was able to make use of her practical help. The case summary gives clear indications of the importance of effective communication in social casework. Because it is a brief summary and not a detailed record, some aspects of communication between client and social worker, and between the social worker and other people are omitted of course. But the illustration provides an adequate basis for further discussion. The summary shows how the medical social worker found it necessary to talk to other people about her client's situation, such as wardens of homes. Other people contacted her—the doctor and the warden of the home to which Mr. Clark applied. Miss Smith and the family doctor might also have been in touch with each other: we are not told this, but Mr. Clark was in touch with the doctor and with his neighbours. It is possible to discuss a communication network and the directions in which communication flowed.

Communication between Mr. Clark and Miss Smith seemed to be effective. Miss Smith seemed to be able to understand something of Mr. Clark's feelings and ideas about his situation. Mr. Clark was able to express his feelings and thoughts and also to communicate them to the social worker. The social worker was able to understand what the client's communications were intended to mean, at least to a sufficient extent to respond appropriately at times. Certain aspects of the social worker's behaviour in the interviews are important. One of these is her listening to what the client said. Another is the way in which she seemed to accept the client's pace so that she did not press him to reveal more than he was prepared to, nor to act before he felt able to. The social worker seemed to convey interest and concern not only in what she said but through other aspects of her behaviour which are not fully described in the summary, although they are always part of the inter-action between two people. Communication between two people occurs not through words alone, but through a combination of media, which include action and gesture and other forms of non-verbal behaviour.

It may be helpful at this point to refer to some experimental work on the expected behaviour of a potentially helpful person. In the case summary it seems that Miss Smith responded appropriately to Mr. Clark's needs and the following analysis may clarify her role as helper. The experimental work (Thomas *et al.*, 1955) identified three kinds of expectation.

The client expected the potentially helpful person to be able to identify and reduce his tension in an initial interview, and to structure the inter-view, overcoming the client's decision-making difficulties regarding the the progress of the interview. In the sphere of communication the helpful person was expected to

(a) assign importance to the problem presented by the client,

(b) show willingness to maintain communication and

(c) show willingness to broaden the range of communications made accessible to both the client and the helper.

Timms (1964) commented that the social worker would be concerned to gain certain impressions of the client, but too great attention to the gathering of information at the expense of attention to the concerns the client is expressing at the time, will produce neither meaningful information, nor the experience of being, at least partially, understood.

4. *Non-verbal behaviour*

Non-verbal behaviour plays an important part in the interaction between social worker and client. In the situation where information is given it might provide the social worker with feedback, indicating whether the information given was understood or not. If, for example, the client looked puzzled this might indicate that he did not understand the information he was given. Non-verbal behaviour might convey more subtle messages. As in the case of verbal communication it might cause confusion to client and social worker because the content of the message was ambiguous or distorted by the sender or receiver. The social worker might communicate concern for and willingness to help the client through non-verbal behaviour, such as providing material or financial resources. Other actions could have the effect of encouraging the client to act differently. Accompanying him on visits to the offices of the Department of Employment and Productivity, or the Ministry of Social Security, or to the hospital, might be helpful if a client was anxious about doing any of these things alone. Such actions might also be helpful because they encouraged the client to try to cope with these situations. Having seen that the social worker coped, the client might feel reassured about attempting to cope himself, and by learning how the social worker behaved, he might learn new ways of behaving himself (for example, in putting forward his point of view in an interview).

An action demonstrates something directly. A gesture represents something—a thought, an idea or a feeling. Gestures are symbols. In seeking to understand gestures, it is helpful to think of some action which has a definite referent so that the action becomes a recognisable symbol. As in the case of words, gestures may be misinterpreted. It is not necessarily correct to assume that because a person nods his head in a certain way, he is making an affirmative sign nor that other forms of behaviour, for example, walking out of a meeting, are intended to be communicative. Some gestures have the same significance as words. Non-verbal gestures must be conventionalised because if they were not they would lack communicative significance. In every society there are many conventional gestures and most people in a given culture know when such gestures are appropriate, how to make them, and what they signify. Some styles of expression are likely to be adopted in childhood. Occasionally there may be vestiges of childhood mannerisms in adulthood. They may give indications of the history of a person's development more than of his current state. Some actions may be performed habitually or without conscious thought. They may still be communicative whether the performer wants them to be or not.

5. *Combinations of media*

In most situations communication takes place through complex media where two or more different media are combined. The simplest conversation combines language, gesture and sound and can easily incorporate action and image as well. By image is meant non-verbal signs such as the clothes a person wears, or the kind of house he lives in. What is often signified by such signs is social status.

Four main channels of human communication may be distinguished. Verbal communication, the use of words, is one. Extra-verbal communication refers to the communication of ideas conveyed by the implied meaning of words as distinct from the logical content of the words, and tone of voice, by which people convey consciously or unconsciously, that the spoken words have two different meanings: the logical and the implied meanings. Human beings also make noises, not in the form of words but as grunts, groans, sighs and so on, which communicate primitive ideas of love, hate, joy, sorrow, pain and fear. Such noises are described as unverbalised phonation. Communication also occurs non-verbally through posture, gesture, and facial expression, through which feeling is communicated. Extra-verbal communication needs to be seen in conjunction with non-verbal communication (Lambrick, 1962).

All but the most primitive communications depend on thought processes and thinking involves the use of words. People may communicate by action or gesture but the purpose of communicating has often been formulated by thought. A great deal of human communication takes place through the medium of verbal language.

But verbal communication is not separate from other media. The transmission of words is only a part of the total message that is being conveyed and received. We have noted that messages are also conveyed by the tone of voice, facial expression and other forms of behaviour so that, apart from language, the basic media of human communication are action, gesture, image, sound, smell and flavour, as we have seen. When a word is spoken the hearer obtains information from two sources. One is information drawn from previous experience of the word which enables him to interpret and evaluate the meaning of the speaker in an objective way. Second, information is obtained from the actual sound of the word irrespective of its objective meaning. The tone of voice gives information about the speaker and may indicate that he has a cold, or is tired or bored by what he is talking about.

6. *Expressive and coping behaviour*

Some actions are performed or are not performed, deliberately in order to communicate something. People express resentment or disapproval by refusing to talk in an interview or by walking out of a meeting. If we wish others to know how we feel and our actions or inactivity are understood by those around us, we may be said to be communicating how we feel. Expression is only one-half of the process of communication. If a person expresses his feelings verbally or non-verbally, and there is no one present to observe his behaviour, he is not communicating with other people but only with himself. Communication consists of the transmission of messages and their reception and interpretation. Expressive behaviour is spontaneous and sometimes uncontrollable. It has no specific aim in the sense of helping a person to cope with his situation although it may incidentally have effects. The term refers to bodily changes, such as blushing or crying, and to a person's manner or style of behaviour. It is also used to describe the conscious and deliberate communication of ideas and feelings.

Coping behaviour may be thought of as the predicate of action (what a person is doing) and expressive behaviour as the adverb of action (how he is doing it). Coping behaviour is purposive and specifically motivated. It is determined by the needs of the moment and by the situation and it is therefore formally elicited. Coping can be more readily controlled (inhibited, modified, or conventionalised) and it usually aims to change the environment. Coping and expression are both present in every act although they are present in unequal proportions. No act can be called purely and solely expressive or purely and solely coping. Every activity, even if heavily loaded with expressiveness, has an origin: it is stimulated. Every act a person performs invariably has these two aspects, the coping and the expressive. Both are important to an understanding of personality. It is important to distinguish what a person thinks (the content of cognition) from his way of thinking (cognitive style). In the same way what a person is trying to do is highly revealing, but so too is his manner of doing it. It is not safe to claim that a given facial expression, a given gesture, or a certain kind of handwriting always signifies a particular personality trait. But the expressive behaviour of a person is perhaps the most important factor in the understanding of personality (Allport, 1965).

7. *Behaviour and attitude change*

If it had been assumed that people are entirely rational and act in a wholly logical manner on the information available to them, all that Miss Smith need have done to induce Mr. Clark to change his attitudes would have been to give him information. The case summary illustrates the fact that the modification of some attributes does not occur in this simple way. The same is true of changes in behaviour. In some circumstances people will not listen to messages which explicitly convey a viewpoint which differs from their own. In other circumstances, for example, where they have great respect for the sender of the message, they listen. Where they listen and the message reaches them they tend to select from it only those facts which are consistent with their previous experience. They ignore the rest. Or they tend to reinterpret the message so that it has a meaning different from the one intended. Even where they accept new information which conflicts with their previous information they will not necessarily act on the new information. It is possible, as in the case of Mr. Clark, to increase a person's knowledge without his opinion being changed (Parry, 1967).

People such as social workers who wish to influence others to change their attitudes, beliefs or behaviour have a choice of methods. They can attempt to influence the perceiving individual directly. They can attempt to alter his environment so that in turn it will alter his perception. They can try to help him to satisfy the needs and emotions which seem to underlie his existing behaviour and at the same time try to help him to find new perspectives and ways of behaving. They can try to provide social support for the individual who adopts new forms of behaviour. Miss Smith seems to have tried to help Mr. Clark to accept the idea of entering a home by examining the situation with him. They talked about it together and Miss Smith tried to understand how Mr. Clark perceived the problem. She also helped him to find a new perspective. The second heart attack led Mr. Clark to see that continuing to live alone could be hazardous and his doctor's advice confirmed this. We have already noted that Miss Smith provided emotional support to Mr. Clark. His relationship with Miss Smith was satisfying. Because it satisfied some emotional needs and helped him to deal with his anxiety, Mr. Clark became more able to cope with the situation in a rational way.

Mr. Clark's case shows how any significant change in the life of an individual tends to introduce some degree of instability or disharmony in the way his activities, attitudes and beliefs are organised. This instability is described as emotional tension. A significant change results in tension because old behaviour is found to be inadequate. A new situation may require the acquisition of new behaviour. Even if a person is willing to give up his old responses for new ones he will be in a state of tension while he unlearns the old responses. Here he will benefit from support from others which can take a variety of forms. If the tension is not dissipated the person remains in a state of maladjustment or frustration. A common consequence is that he returns to the old responses that he had begun to abandon. If he has a strong wish to change then the successful resolution of his tensions is quicker and more likely; in these circumstances there are fewer returns to old and undesired responses. There may be less tension and reluctance to change if ways are found of dealing with his recognised difficulties. Explanation and logical interpretation alone are often ineffective in changing behaviour because their application is blocked by the emotional satisfaction which a person achieves through his current mode of life. New knowledge can be put to use only as the old behaviour, beliefs and attitudes are unlearned and appropriate new behaviour is learned. An effective way to encourage the learning of new behaviour and attitudes is by consistent prompt attachment of some form of satisfaction to them. This may take the form of consistent praise, approval, strengthened integration with one's group, or material reward. This is particularly important when the desired change is such that the advantages are slow to materialise (Brown, 1963).

8. *Conclusion*

Casework may be considered as essentially a continued exercise in communication. The process has two aspects neither of which can be separated from the other: (1) rapport between social worker and client which can occur without any words being spoken and which is a matter of feeling and (2) an ordering, structuring process that must operate at some level if the experience of one person is to be conveyed to another (Irvine, 1955). An essential feature of communication is the sharing and structuring of experience through the use of verbal and non-verbal symbols. It is a purposeful activity directed towards goals such as affecting people and events. The staff of social agencies are often able to help people by giving them information and advice and material help. Sometimes, because a situation is complicated and because a person has to adjust to changed circumstances, more help than this is needed. Emotional support and the opportunity for discussion of a client's situation may help him to make a new adjustment. The social worker may find it necessary to contact other people in order to provide the service which the client requires. It may be necessary to involve other people directly in helping him. In Mr. Clark's case the medical social worker was in contact with wardens of homes, and probably the family doctor, and discussed her client's situation with them. Mr. Clark was himself in contact with the doctor and with his neighbours, and later with the warden of a home. The medical social worker and Mr. Clark were in different positions in the network of communication. The network itself played an essential part in the helping process: it was important for the social worker to be aware of Mr. Clark's network because his communications with others were an important influence on Mr. Clark. By enlarging his network, for example, through putting him in contact with the wardens of homes, the medical social worker opened up further possibilities of influence both on Mr. Clark by other people and by Mr. Clark himself (for example in asking them to admit him to a home).

Communication is an essential feature of all these activities. There are different channels or means of communication. In a general sense all acts may be regarded as potentially communicative; the expressive behaviour of a person is perhaps the most important factor in the understanding of personality. Human communication usually involves a combination of media.

As a rule a person's behaviour and attitudes change only to the minimal extent that is called for by the demands of his immediate situation. But when a person is confronted by a situation to which he cannot adjust with emotional satisfaction, and which he cannot explain to himself, he is impelled to seek a new adjustment which relieves his emotional tension. People are able to make such adjustments, the nature of the adjustments being dependent on a variety of factors. There are ways of encouraging and assisting the learning of new behaviour and attitudes. Their effectiveness too depends on a range of variables in the person's situation.

At present many of the processes described above are obscure and subjects of controversy. However, there are implications for the conduct of interviews and indications about measures which it may be helpful for social workers to employ. For example, the importance of listening and observation, and the necessity for clear information giving, have been discussed on the assumption that these activities are not simple nor easy to undertake. A number of factors which influence the relationship

CHAPTER 3

Some Influences on Communication between Client and Social Worker

1. *Case illustration: interview between Mrs. Mead and Miss Cross*

The following case illustration forms a basis for the discussion of communication and interpersonal perception which are the subjects of this chapter.

John went to a children's home when he was 2 weeks old and remained there until the age of 4 when his mother remarried. He then returned home but his mother was unable to care for him properly and he went to a foster home. His mother, Mrs. Mead, saw him regularly while he was there. At the age of 7 he had to be admitted to another children's home and his mother again stopped visiting him. She was exempt from making a financial contribution towards his care and the following interview was one of a number made by Miss Cross, Child Care officer, who kept the home situation under review.

Although Mrs. Mead had known Miss Cross since John was in the foster home, she was not at all welcoming, inviting her into the house in an abrupt way, and carrying on with her cooking. She did not look directly at Miss Cross but spoke in an affectionate way to her 3-year-old daughter who was playing on the kitchen floor. The little girl looked shabby and dirty but seemed contented.

Miss Cross breaks a long silence by saying: "I have come to ask about your situation again. As you know we are required to keep in touch with parents whose children are in homes."

31

Mrs. Mead: "Don't give me that, what you've really come for is to see if we'll take the boy back. We've talked about it many times before and I've told you we couldn't cope with him as well. Our flat is too small: there's hardly room for the three of us. Can you tell me where we could put a bed for John? There's hardly room to swing a cat in here."

Miss Cross: "That is just what you said last time I visited you. So there has been no change in the situation."

Mrs. Mead: "Definitely no. If that's all you wanted you could have saved yourself the bother. There was no need for you to come."

Miss Cross: "There is something else I am concerned about . . . "

Mrs. Mead: "Oh yes."

Miss Cross: " . . . and that is why you do not go to see your son."

Mrs. Mead: "You can't make me go and its nobody else's business except ours whether we go or don't go."

Miss Cross: "But after all, Mrs. Mead, you are John's mother. I think that any child is very disappointed if his mother never goes to see him."

Mrs. Mead: "Don't try to persuade me like that. He is far too stupid to understand anything about it."

Miss Cross: "How can you possibly talk like that? Don't you love him?"

Mrs. Mead: "I suppose you think I am a bad mother but why should I risk upsetting my husband and daughter. Surely homes are for children like John."

Miss Cross: "I won't say what I think about that, but couldn't you at least write to him now and then, for example, on his birthday?"

Mrs. Mead: "There'd be no point in that because he couldn't read it— I told you he's stupid. Anyway I don't mean much to John—we don't get on with each other. I don't want him to spoil our family life. Why don't you leave me in peace and let me get on with the cooking?"

Miss Cross feels she is getting nowhere and the interview terminates. She still feels angry and does not want to have to visit Mrs. Mead again.

In this interview we can see how two people communicated their feelings of irritation with each other, and probably their personal dislike of each other too. The previous interviews between Mrs. Mead and Miss Cross had probably contributed to the build up of their defensive

reactions which are evident in this account of the interview. The interview illustrates some of the points made in the previous chapter about
the way non-verbal and verbal behaviour combine in communication.
Some non-verbal cues at the beginning of the visit seem to be significant,
and we can attempt to surmise how Miss Cross interpreted them. To a
great extent what follows will be speculation and no doubt different
people would make different interpretations. This point in particular is
part of the subject matter of this chapter.

Mrs. Mead's behaviour when she opens the door to the social worker,
her direction of gaze, facial expression and posture, all seem to indicate
that she did not welcome the visit. She did not look directly at Miss
Cross, she made no welcoming gestures and she was curt when she said
the worker could enter; we may reasonably assume that she did not
smile. She seemed to invite Miss Cross into the house in a grudging way:
she seemed to speak in a "hostile tone of voice". Her manner towards
Miss Cross seems to have contrasted with the affectionate way in which
she spoke to the child. Miss Cross noticed this, and that she carried on
with her cooking at the stove. This appeared to indicate that the visit
was made at an inconvenient time for Mrs. Mead because she was busy
with the household tasks. Perhaps, because of her attitude towards Mrs.
Mead, the social worker had not informed her in advance that she would
be making the visit. Perhaps Miss Cross's "reason" was that she would
obtain a more adequate assessment of the home situation if she called
without warning. There may be many "reasons" but it is clear that the
social worker said she was making the visit because she was required to:
she was empowered to inquire about the situation. This message can be
interpreted in a number of ways. It seems that it could mean that Miss
Cross felt that she must justify her visit to herself and to Mrs. Mead.
Perhaps she felt she must demonstrate that she had authority, as a way of
protecting herself from Mrs. Mead's resentment of her as a person.
Perhaps she felt a need to "sort out" or "tidy up" a situation which did
not coincide with her notions of "good family life".

There are observations of a little girl who looked shabby and dirty
and who seems happy and contented. Miss Cross may have given more
weight to the child's dirty appearance and less weight to her apparent
happiness. This selective observation would be congruent with a later

verbal message to the effect that Mrs. Mead is a bad mother. For some people an alternative interpretation might place more weight on the observation that the child seems happy. The child's happiness might be seen as an indication of the quality of her family life or her relationship with her mother. It would be incongruent with the view of Mrs. Mead as a bad mother.

I think that it is easy to feel irritated by Miss Cross, as Mrs. Mead did. One's instinctive reaction can be to say that Miss Cross was a "bad" social worker and that this was a "bad" interview. This kind of instinctive reaction to the message contained in the account of the interview carries the danger that, because we feel unsympathetic towards the social worker, further attempts at understanding the situation may be blocked. You may not share this reaction. You may find other cues in the evidence which lead you to see the situation differently. Many social workers, including the writer, may have found themselves behaving as Miss Cross did, or in ways very similar. Many social workers experience conflict in exercising authority. These specualtive comments, controversial as they may be, do however serve to introduce discussion of important influences on communication in the dyad and in larger groups. They indicate that communications are transmitted, received and interpreted on different levels—for example the level of content—of what is said and its literal meaning—and the level of interpretation of how it is said. This reminds us of the cues from non-verbal behaviour which we have discussed.

If we turn to the verbal messages that were sent during the interview it is possible to interpret these on different levels. The social worker's opening remark, for example, carries implications beyond what she actually said. In saying that she was required to inquire about Mrs. Mead's situation she was hinting that she had the support or sanction of authority for her inquiry. She was also saying that she was checking whether the exemption from financial contributions for John's case should continue. It seems that Mrs. Mead receives this message since she seems to know that she could be required to take John back. It is evident that past experience is an important factor here.

The social worker does not respond by asking Mrs. Mead more about the inability to cope if John came home. She thus misses an opportunity to encourage Mrs. Mead to talk about a topic of concern to her and which

Mrs. Mead might have found it helpful to talk about. It would be incorrect to suggest that it is surprising that the social worker missed this opportunity. We have already observed that the social worker's perception of the situation and of her own role in it was one which would prevent her from conveying "acceptance" of and openness towards Mrs. Mead. There is striking evidence that the social worker's attitude led Mrs. Mead to respond defensively throughout the interview and sometimes the social worker reveals her attitude as if by accident. For example, at one stage she refuses to make a comment about Mrs. Mead's unwillingness to visit John. This refusal itself could be thought to convey a hint that she disapproves. Her attempt to persuade the mother to visit John could also be interpreted as an implied criticism of Mrs. Mead's behaviour, the message here being "how can you disappoint your child in this way?" This forces the mother to rationalise her behaviour by reference to her son's supposed inability to understand. Incidentally this remark shifts the topic from one of feeling to an intellectual one— understanding.

When the mother says that she herself "does not mean much to John", on one level this could represent an appeal for understanding of real difficulties in their relationship, on another, as a further attempt to justify not having John home, and on another as an appeal for reassurance that John did miss her and wanted to be with her. It is interesting to question why the interview became focused on John's coming home and on contact between mother and son in the way that it did. Perhaps the most striking feature of the conversation is the way in which areas for discussion progressively and quickly became narrower and narrower as each person became more angry. Instead of encouraging the "opening up" of topics the social worker's communications have the effect of shifting the conversation from one point to another in a negative or unconstructive way.

2. *Obstacles to communication between social worker and client*

It may be helpful at this point to describe an American study of factors which seemed to contribute to communication problems between clients and social workers at intake interviews. It suggests how such problems may be studied by groups of social workers and is useful in suggesting the kinds of influence which such groups might consider. A group of social workers in a family service agency in the United States attempted to evaluate case material by means of group study (Stark, 1959). The cases were selected on one simple criterion, namely that the social worker considered that the client was difficult to engage in exploring his problem. The study was not a formal research project and the cases were not selected on a statistical basis.

Discussion was focused on the problem areas in both the client's attitudes and behaviour and the social worker's activity. Only cases that had no prior contact with the agency were included in the study since it seemed advisable to rule out consideration of client attitudes that derived from past agency experience. All the intake interviews of the cases selected were reviewed and the reports on the interviews were read by all members of the study group prior to discussion. A total of twenty cases was studied. In five of these two family members were interviewed making a total of twenty-five clients. In the opinion of the study group only two of the clients manifested attitudes and behaviour that could be characterised as genuinely resistive. In the other eighteen cases it seemed that the clients would be able to use help provided the social workers were able to understand the framework within which the clients viewed their problems. It was thought that in the main, the social workers' difficulties did not stem from lack of a basic knowledge of personality theory but rather from errors in application of knowledge and techniques. It was apparent in the group discussions of the cases that the social workers were generally able, in retrospect, to see their faulty application of theory.

The social workers seemed to have difficulty in three major areas: (1) in identifying the clients' characteristically defensive responses, (2) in obtaining a full and clear statement of the presenting request and (3) in responding in an unstereotyped fashion to the client's presentations. The difficulties the social workers encountered in obtaining an understanding of the presenting request fell into four categories: (1) the tendency to shift the focus away from the client's concern when the material was bizarre or markedly inconsistent, (2) the failure to structure the interview for clarity when the client presented rambling, diffuse material without defining his "problem", (3) unwarranted expressions of "understanding" in an effort to hold the client and (4) identifying with one aspect of a client's ambivalence and thereby failing to hear all that was said and to evaluate the conflict accurately.

A number of stereotyped responses by the social workers were evident in the cases studied. These seemed to be based on certain misconceptions of the roles of the client and social worker. In a number cases it was evident that the social worker was unduly direct in focusing on the client's part in creating his difficulties. The expectation seemed to be that the client could drop his projections merely by having his attention called to his own part in the problem. The misconception that social workers must not give advice seemed to be applied in a number of cases. The social workers sometimes appeared to be so afraid to deal with specific requests for advice that they became rigid in their responses almost to the point of being authoritative in the interview. This was an interesting contradiction in the social worker's tendency to underplay the role of authority. Another example of a stereotyped response was the giving of a routine and intellectual explanation of the agency's functions and services, instead of an explanation that had meaning for the client and in language understandable to him. The misconception that all clients had some knowledge and acceptance of the purposes of social agencies created barriers between social worker and client. It was obvious that social workers must take into account the probability that clients from various cultures would have varying degrees of knowledge about social work services. For some clients social agencies were equated with authoritative organisations.

3. *Interpersonal perception*

The material presented so far leads us to consider how social worker and client perceive each other and their situation. How does interpersonal perception influence communication? What influence does communication have on interpersonal perception? It is impossible to separate these processes in everyday life but for purposes of study we have to try to analyse them. Perception is the process by which we become aware of and interpret our sensations about the world around us. Many different factors influence our perceptions such as the cues from the stimulus, the context, the experiences we have derived from the past, our inherited abilities, and the many motives, needs and drives at the moment of perception (Munn, 1961). In other words, people "see" things differently. "Facts" may be seen quite differently by different people. An important determinant of a person's view of the world is the relevance of what is perceived to his own needs.

The responses of the individual to persons and things are shaped by the way they appear to him—his cognitive world. Every person has an individual image or "map" of the world. This "map" may be described as a schema, a word which is useful for describing experience organised in fairly well-defined patterns. Experience organised in less well-defined ways (such as "attitude to sex") may be indicated by the term "assumption". The process of perception is selective and interpretative. The information that a person gets from the outer world depends on stimulus factors, such as the context or total situation, and the frequency and intensity of stimulation and factors which derive from the characteristics of the perceiving individual such as his emotions, needs and past experience which are organised in schemata. Human relationships play an important role in perception. They have contributed to the formation, testing and modifying of the individual's schemata and they are often a significant part of the context.

The difference between perceiving people and perceiving other objects is discussed by Allport (1963). Human objects, unlike others, impress perceivers with their purposes, their animation, their intentions towards others, and their relative unpredictability. In appraising another a person usually has a special reason in view such as matching him to a situation—seeing if he can perform a task or fill a particular role. Because of this a person is likely to be perceived in a special and therefore not a comprehensive way. The results include halo effects, and stereotyping. If you have a generally favourable impression of another person this impression will tend to spread to your appraisal of specific personality traits: you will tend to judge him too high on desirable traits. In the case of an unfavourable impression the tendency may be to rate undesirable traits too highly. Stereotyping is the tendency to attribute to an individual, traits which we assume characterise his group. The danger of stereotypes is that they may blind us to the many individual differences among the members of any groups, although a stereotype is not necessarily a source of error. But the chief obstacle to accurate judgement of people still lies in the tendency to oversimplify perceptions of persons.

In addition to our perceptions of others our perceptions of ourselves are important. We have a need for a distinct and consistent self-image and a need for self-esteem. We may seek to obtain from others responses which confirm our attitudes towards ourselves. To protect and enhance ourselves we try to manipulate the picture other people have of us by putting up a front that will make them think we are what we wish to be. The problem is that other people are acting, too, in a similar way and this can make communication difficult. The roles taken by people may provide a solution to the problem of ego identity. For example, in seeing himself primarily in terms of his occupation a man has a clear public identity to adopt. He may laugh a little at the role to indicate to others that really there is more to him than can be seen just in this role (Goffman, 1956).

4. *Cognitive processes and the concept of the schema*

Perception is one of the cognitive processes. Cognition is a general term covering all the various ways of knowing: perceiving, remembering, imaging, conceiving, judging, reasoning (Drever, 1952). A cognitive system is an interrelated complex of separate cognitions about objects and persons. These cognitive systems direct the individual's social actions. One of the most important kinds of cognitive system is the causal system, the perception of two objects or events in a cause and effect relationship. In a new or ambiguous situation the immediate perception of cause and effect is largely determined by the temporal coincidence of two events. Cognitive consonance refers to the internal harmony existing among the components of a cognitive system. A cognitive system is high in consonance when its component cognitions are congruent and low in consonance when they are incongruent or contradictory. A state of balance exists in a cognitive system to the extent that the elements of the system form units which have non-contradictory relationships. A non-contradictory relationship is one in which each element is harmonious with the other elements. Unbalanced cognitive systems tend to shift towards a state of balance. A person attempts to perceive, cognise or evaluate the various aspects of his environment and of himself in such a way that the behavioural implications of his perceptions shall not be contradictory.

The idea of the schema is helpful in understanding how past experience predisposes a person to behave in certain ways rather than others, or how old information is related to new information. In coping with life people sometimes seem to behave as though searching for impressions or models which past experiences have left and adapting them to new experiences. Schemas have been described as persistent, deep-rooted and well-organised classifications of ways of perceiving, thinking and behaving. The schema is modified by learning and influences other schemas. Its purpose is to supply a working model of some aspect of the world. Schemas may be thought of as relating to emotional reactions as well as intellectual abstractions. Schemas are therefore of help to people in seeing, evaluating and responding to situations. They may also contribute to an inability to see certain things if the schema into which a person fits a new experience is an inappropriate one (Abercrombie, 1969).

If we are to get a full picture of an individual's outlook, and so of the communications he is likely to make and the interpretations he will put upon those he receives, we must bear in mind the many cognitive and emotional schemas which he has evolved. Cognitive schemas tend to have an objective orientation whereas emotional schemas are necessarily related to the person's preferences and aversions. The first are likely to be modified in relation to environmental change while the second will bend the environment to their own image. When the schemas of two people are incompatible, the emotional kind are likely to produce the greater barriers to communication.

5. *Emotional schemata*

Study of the interview between Mrs. Mead and Miss Cross provides illustrations of emotional barriers to communication. We noted, for example, that because each person needed to protect herself she tended to attack the other. Attack is often seen as being a form of defence, although this platitude is often expressed in a more sophisticated manner. Psycho-analytic theory has made a considerable contribution to social work and we will now review briefly some ideas relevant to the present discussion. We can then proceed to study some complexities which so far have not been discussed very explicitly. Two psycho-analytic concepts, important to social workers interested in motivation, and also important in the study of communication, are anxiety and threats to the ego. The idea of the unconscious has led to important changes in thinking about motivation. Ego threats are important because of their consequences, the defence mechanisms such as regression, aggression and repression. What has been learned about unusual perceptual distortions, hallucinations and amnesias has influenced the study of ordinary perception. Emotional factors, whether positive or negative, may lead to selective and distorted perceptions. The chief mechanisms responsible for these selections and distortions are the means by which the ego protects itself from the consequences of the feelings.

Rationalisation functions to defend the ego against feelings of guilt. It involves finding a justifiable excuse or alibi in the external world for doing something that is frowned on by the super-ego. It may involve substituting a socially approved motive for a socially disapproved one. Rationalisation is thus the process by which a person justifies his action by reasoning after the event. Projection is said to occur when a person interprets the behaviour of another in terms of his own unconscious needs and impulses. As a receiver of information he is prone to slant his interpretation in accordance with his desires and fears.

Interpretation plays an important part in the receipt of information. Attempts to account for some aspects of the external world usually contain a projective element. An individual tends to try to explain the behaviour of other people in terms of his own experience and reactions. Identification is a process by which a person unconsciously or partly unconsciously behaves, or imagines himself behaving, as if he were the person with whom he has a close emotional tie. When a person projects his own motives on to another's behaviour he identifies that person with

D

himself. If a person sides vehemently with another he is said to be identified with that person or his situation. When this occurs he will reject
information inconsistent with the case to which he feels committed.

The process of repression can lead to the full rejection of unwelcome
information. It occurs when impulses and desires are in conflict with
enforced standards of conduct. The impulses, desires and associated
memories and thoughts, and the painful emotions arising out of the
conflict, are thrust out of consciousness into the unconscious. They
remain active in the unconscious and play an indirect part in determining
behaviour, dreams and neurotic symptoms. The person behaves as if
he has not heard or seen material too painful to be recognised or which is
incompatible with a securely held belief (Hilgard and Bower, 1966).

In psycho-analysis the concept of one person rather than persons in
relationship is central. A person or subject is thought of as existing and
functioning as the centre of a world consisting of himself and his object
to whom he relates by complicated processes and manipulations. In
relationships between two individuals they are each both subject and
object. Each is a subject in his own right but each is also the object of
the other. The adaptive and defensive processes of each person are geared
in with those of the other, and have to function in relation to the other.
A person responds to others not only in terms of his own feelings and
perceptions but also in terms of what he perceives the other's responses
and assumptions about himself to be. A person anticipates the response
of the other to his own behaviour. This is modified by his anticipations
and assumptions about the other. This whirling circle of phantasies and
perceptions has been called the spiral of reciprocal perspectives (Laing
et al., 1966). We will now go on to consider some further social influences
on communication behaviour and some aspects of family and group
interaction.

CHAPTER 4

Social Factors in Communication

1. Perception and primary groups

Individuals are very much influenced by their primary groups in their perception of events. When an individual holds an opinion different from one held by his reference or membership group he tends to change it so as to conform to the group because such conformity is regarded as maximising his chances to achieve his goals as an individual. Even where a person feels in a position to decide certain issues for himself he is still more likely to be influenced by communications which are consistent with his group norms. Opinions and actions are generally much more public than information-gathering processes. The attainment of knowledge is generally a more private form of behaviour than the expression of opinion or action. Because group tolerance for these different forms of behaviour varies it is quite possible that people may change their states of knowledge without changing their actions or their opinions.

2. Social control

Leonard (1966) has discussed the sociological view of social work as a mechanism of social control. The processes by which society secures conformity to its expectations include coercion, employed by agencies of law and government and accomplished by force or the threatened use of force, and by persuasion which operates to induce an individual to respond to the norms of a larger social group. Social work agencies may exercise a mixture of coercion and persuasion but all agencies, even

43

those whose powers appear to be entirely persuasive, are concerned with the modification of human behaviour in the direction of certain cultural norms.

3. *Family tasks and role distribution*

The family is a social group which exists to satisfy the needs of its members and to perform certain essential tasks from the point of view of society. In modern industrial society the family is the chief means of socialising children and maintaining the socialisation of adults. The family evolves a series of role relationships which will be modified as family tasks alter—for example, as the children grow up and the parents and children grow older (Timms, 1964). Different families will have different ways of carrying out their tasks. Roles will be distributed differently in these various families. In one kind of family parental responsibilities are carried jointly by mother and father. In theory this implies that the children are likely to be secure in their relationships with their parents and friction between siblings is likely to be minimal. In another kind of family father is dominant, and the roles of mother and children too may be clearly defined. Alternatively, mother may be dominant. Both parents may seek to avoid the dominant position. This may be an insecure situation for the children in which case it will be the least favourable type of family structure.

The stability of the family hinges on the extent to which the needs of the members are met and roles are compatible or complementary, rather than antagonistic. Role complementarity may break down. One or both parents, for example, may be ignorant or unfamiliar with the required roles. There may be conflict about a person's right to a role he wishes to play. Family members may have conflicting perceptions of their roles (Spiegel, 1961). Cultural differences in the backgrounds of family members may underlie differences in expectations and in role functioning.

Three different ideas about the usage of the term role can be distinguished. A "prescribed role" consists of a system of expectations which exist in social life, surrounding the occupant of a position. People have expectations about his behaviour towards the occupants of other positions. The "subjective role" refers to the expectations which an individual has about his own behaviour in interaction with other people. An "enacted role" consists of the behaviour of an occupant of a position when he interacts with occupants in other positions. What is meant by role thus depends on the position from which a person's behaviour is observed. In a group the various roles are interdependent. A person's role, generally speaking, is what he is appointed, or expected, or has undertaken to do and to feel like. Social roles are defined in terms of other people's actions and feelings in relation to the occupant of a given position (Perlman, 1966).

4. *Patterns of communication in families*

Berne (1966) describes each unit of social intercourse, such as a conversation, as a transaction. People may open a transaction from any of three positions towards any three of his partner's positions. These ego-positions are three ego-states denoted in Berne's terminology as Child, Adult or Parent. For Berne, Child and Parent ego-states are present in each person. These transactions may be described on a diagram and they may be classified as complementary or crossed, simple or ulterior, and ulterior transactions may be divided into angular or duplex types. This classification of interaction patterns is important in studying communication and can be thought of as ways of distinguishing relationships based on equality or difference. In the first case, the partners tend to mirror each other's behaviour. This is symmetrical interaction and it is characterised by quality and the minimising of difference. In the second case the partner's behaviour complements that of the other. Complementary interaction is based on the maximisation of difference. One partner may occupy a superior position and the other the inferior, subordinate position. These positions may be socially defined as in the doctor–patient or mother–child relationships to take two common examples. One partner does not necessarily impose a complementary relationship on the other; each partner behaves in a manner which presupposes, or takes for granted, the behaviour of the other. Their definitions of the relationship thus coincide.

Ulterior transactions involve the activity of more than two ego states simultaneously. Angular transactions involve three ego-states. Berne gives this example:

Salesman: "This one is better but you can't afford it."

Housewife: "That's the one I'll take."

In saying that one object is better and that the housewife cannot afford it the salesman is talking at the social level to the Adult of the housewife. The Adult reply would be that he was correct about both points. But the salesman is also communicating on a psychological or ulterior level to the housewife's Child. Her Child's reply says in effect: "Regardless of the financial consequences I'll show him that I'm as good as any of his customers." At both levels the transaction is complementary.

A duplex ulterior transaction involves four ego-states. It is conducted both on an Adult level and on a Child level by both partners and is commonly seen in flirtations. It differs from the angular transaction illustrated above, where the salesman remains in the Adult state throughout.

Patterns of communication may be similar or different for different family members, or they may be pervasive in the family unit. Forms of communicative behaviour may be primarily for attack or defence; some communications will be provocative or a reaction to provocation. Patterns of communication may reflect the way in which the neurotic needs of one individual or the interlocking neurotic needs of various individuals are met in the family. Basing their approach on psycho-analytic ideas the Family Discussion Bureau (Bannister *et al.*, 1955) seeks in its work to understand the processes of unconscious collusion between husband and wife—how far marital stress may be seen as an expression of the phantasies of the partners, how far the responses of partners to each other and to their children are influenced by their relations with parents and siblings in earlier life. Because of her unconscious needs a mother may unwittingly (or deliberately) provoke certain behaviour on the part of her child and also plays a part in perpetuating it because of her own unresolved conflicts. Often, the problems of a family member are the external signs of the problems of the group.

5. *Incongruence between levels of communication*

Some communications may have the effect of maintaining the equilibrium of a group through containing the anxiety of group members. There is a distinctive style of communication which, in an extreme form, is thought to characterise the families of schizophrenic patients. In a less extreme form it is a common experience. The key to understanding this distinctive style is that communication occurs on two levels and often on more than two. Bateson, Jackson and their associates (Weakland, 1960) consider this process to play a significant part in the development of schizophrenia. One level of communication is that of the content itself—what is said. The second level in some way qualifies what is said—affirms it, denies it, indicates that what is said is serious or a joke, is a suggestion or a command, etc. The first level of communication is ordinarily the level of words; the second is ordinarily that of vocal intonation and bodily gesture. The schizophrenic is a person who grows up in a family in which what is said is typically qualified in such a way as to be incongruent. The mother may characteristically address her child as "dear" but in a tone of voice which conveys hostility. If the child attempts to comment on the incongruence between these two levels the mother may resort to a third level of communication and deny that there was any incongruence in her mode of behaviour.

The child, because of his dependency and need for love, cannot leave and thus escape from the pain of having to cope continually with these incongruent messages. His parents do not permit him to comment on their communicative behaviour in a way that would induce them toward greater congruence between levels. As a result of growing up in this prevailing double-bind situation the child who later becomes schizophrenic suffers an impaired capacity to discriminate correctly communication modes within himself and between self and others. This is because, for the subject, the double bind consists of a pattern of distorted or ambiguous communication with one or several members of his family. This situation can destroy the validity of the feelings that normally guide and adjust behaviour in interpersonal situations. This distorted way of communicating leads to a blurring of roles in the family, and a confusion of identity. Such communication is common. In growing up children have to learn which of two contradictory messages to choose. But if a child is surrounded by a number of people who communicate with him in this way continually he may develop a chronic inability to judge which of the two sides of a contradictory communication to respond to.

Perhaps the most frequent form of this kind of communication is through an injunction demanding specific behaviour which by its very nature can only be spontaneous. Anyone faced with this injunction is in an untenable position because to comply he would have to be spontaneous and to comply with a demand at the same time. Here are some examples of these injunctions to be spontaneous. "You ought to love me." "I want you to dominate me." "You should enjoy playing with the children just like other fathers." "Don't be so obedient."

An essential ingredient of the double-bind situation is the prohibition to be aware of the contradiction involved. Because of this the subject may conclude that either he is overlooking vital clues inherent in the situation or offered him by significant others. He may be forced to extend his search to the most unlikely and unrelated phenomena. He may comply with any or all injunctions with complete literalness and thus appear foolish. He may withdraw, by blocking the input channels of communication (perceptual defence) by appearing to be unapproachable or unresponsive, or by engaging in intense activity so as to blot out all incoming messages (Laing, 1965).

It can be seen that this kind of analysis does not treat communication as a self-contained system of behaviour but attempts to view communication, perception, thinking and fantasy as interrelated aspects of experience and behaviour.

6. *The family and socialisation*

It is also apparent that to talk simply of child-rearing practices carries the risk of too narrow a conception of the family's task of socialisation. The whole family affects, and is affected by, each of its members. Children and parents contribute to the socialisation of each other. We should therefore bear in mind that within the family members influence each other but it may be helpful to simplify the situation in order to study this question of influence further. Thus the importance of the family's task of socialisation does not lie solely in securing adherence to parental demands, or in the transmission of the parents' values to the child. But the parents do transmit social influences. As far as "society" is concerned, socialisation requires the production of people with the appropriate abilities and in approximately the right numbers to fill roles in society. Society needs a range of different kinds of people some of whose roles will be incompatible with those of others. Child-rearing practices contribute to the meeting of a variety of needs.

A second aspect of socialisation is the transmission of information from the older generation to the younger. Some of this information will be required for the playing of particular roles. Some people learn some information: no one person learns it all. A third aspect of socialisation is the development of motives and values that contribute to the cohesiveness of society, or sections of society. A society will be more stable if people obtain satisfaction and enjoyment out of performing their roles. Socialisation helps people learn to feel valuable in their roles. The transmission of common values contributes to the modification of individual motivations and the prevention of social disharmony.

Parsons and Bales (1955) have analysed the socialisation process and this account is based on their work. It will be seen that one of its important features is the emphasis on socialisation as an activity of an entire social system. Families need to be studied as units or systems within larger social systems. It is probably impossible to isolate the development of one family member from other family variables although some developmental processes—learned behaviour, defence mechanisms—can be studied individualistically.

Children learn about social and cultural norms directly, for example, through the observation of the behaviour of family members and indirectly through learning about concealed implications of their parents' attitudes. They are not only exposed to information opinions and attitudes obtained from people with whom they are in face-to-face contact. They also make use of other means of communication such as books, comics, radio and television. Because much that is written about the supposed influence of the mass media on children says or implies that it is adverse, the benefits may be overlooked. Children and adults may benefit from being better informed than they were before, for example. The use that the individual makes of the media of communication depends on himself. In general it seems that people look for repetition of their existing experiences into which they can project themselves rather than new experiences in the mass media (Katz and Lazarsfeld, 1955).

Studies which have been made of the possible connection between television violence and delinquency suggest that, although such influences may, in themselves, be undesirable, there is no clear evidence of any effect on normal children. They may have a different effect on already maladjusted children. The available evidence is slight but maladjusted children show a marked preference for such material, derive distinctive satisfactions from it and their problems are sustained rather than resolved in the process of consumption (Brown, 1963).

Personal contact seems to be more effective in influencing people to change their attitudes than the mass media. The mass media seem to be ineffective in changing attitudes over short periods of time; this seems to be largely due to the fact that people select information which is congruent with their existing attitudes. Face-to-face persuasion is more flexible; the communicator can change his message to suit the resistance of the audience and people are more likely to trust someone they know rather than an impersonal mass communication. Opinion leaders may transmit ideas presented on radio or television and thus influence other people: the influence of the mass media may thus be indirect (Katz and Lazarsfeld, 1955).

7. *Language, culture and social class*

The study of family and small group process is a subject in itself with its own special problems and conceptual difficulties which are described by such authorities as Ackerman (1958), Pollak (1960), Scherz (1963), and Coyle (1965). In this brief review I have attempted to describe some important aspects of family interaction. The idea of role distribution in social groups is helpful in social work practice (Perlman, 1966) and in seeking to understand communication processes in groups. Some distinctive styles of communication in families illustrate how communication occurs on different levels. The idea of role ascription and assumption, though a complex topic, invites consideration of the family's tasks of child rearing and socialisation. It opens the way to considering how cultural norms and influences are transmitted, and the influence of social class on perception and communication behaviour.

Culture means the material and behavioural arrangements which have been adopted by a society as the traditional ways of solving the problems of its members. Underlying social institutions are cultural beliefs, norms, and values which govern conduct. These cultural beliefs include the ideas and knowledge, myths and legends, which are shared by the members of a society or by the typical occupants of various positions in a society. Culture is created and transmitted. Language helps make this possible since it facilitates the communication of meaning and the sharing of experiences among people. Communication, regarded as the interchange of meanings among people, occurs mainly through language and language reflects both the personality of the individual and the culture of his society. Language helps in the formation of lasting societies. It makes continuity possible, for example, through the maintenance of written records, and it contributes to the effective functioning and control of social groups. The extent to which language has a significant influence on the development and change of a culture remains controversial. Whorf's hypothesis that the language of a society not only reflects but determines its ideas has received support and it does seem that some languages are more public (or restricted) and suited to social and concrete purposes while others are more formal (or elaborated) and suited to abstract thinking.

The language behaviour of the individual, like other central aspects of his behaviour, necessarily reflects basic features of his personality. His language behaviour, having been developed in the context of his particular culture, necessarily reflects basic features of that culture. The specific language which the individual uses helps to determine his mental processes and thus helps to govern the development of his personality. Sapir (1921) said that people see and hear and otherwise experience

largely as they do because the language habits of their community pre-
dispose them to certain choices of interpretation. Each people evolves
a language which is adequate for handling its own range of problems.
People in different cultures perceive the world in basically different ways.
Whorf (1956) assumed that differences in linguistic form indicated differences in ways of perceiving and organising reality. He noted that
Eskimos have three words for three different kinds of snow for which
there are no English equivalents.

The findings of a number of workers studying social differences in
child-rearing practices, and in particular, in the use of language are
complementary (Bernstein, 1965; Douglas, 1964; Newson and Newson,
1968). They attach high importance to the importance of verbal communication in the process of socialisation as both supporting and interpreting parental example. Middle-class parents tend to use words in
maintaining discipline, and to interact generally with their children in a
more verbally articulate way than lower working-class parents. Working-
class parents tend to avoid lengthy discussion of actions—theirs or the
child's—and, in controlling their children, prefer methods which produce
quick results. This style of control emphasises adult authority, exerted
through physical coercion. The working-class child is relatively unin-
hibited in the direct expression of his feelings and reacts overtly to frustration. He imitates the way adults react to him when he annoys them and
has not been taught to hold back from expressing his feelings. The
middle-class child, by contrast, internalises the moral values and prohi-
bitions of his culture and is controlled in his conduct by his own guilt
feelings. His parents tend to discipline more by psychological methods,
by talking about misbehaviour, and arousing guilt feelings, pointing out
the consequences of the child's actions. The middle-class child thus turns
aggression in on himself and reacts to conflict situations by repression.
The working-class child tends to use denial and displacement and is
more likely to blame the environment rather than himself. The middle-
class culture emphasises delayed gratification—the Reality principle as
against the Pleasure principle in contrast to the working-class culture.
There is a danger that these generalisations are oversimplified and do
not do justice to a wide range of patterns of family interaction and socialisation. Care is needed, too, in analysing factors influencing these

differences. It may be that some children at the lower end of the social scale have more limited verbal experience mainly because of their parents' poor linguistic ability, and consequent difficulty in communicating with them adequately. But in many cases lack of skill may not be a major factor. Other factors, such as emotion, attitude or situation, may be of greater significance (Newson and Newson, 1968). Bernstein's work will now be discussed in more detail.

Bernstein (1958, 1959, 1965) (Lawton, 1968) has provided a comprehensive theoretical account of the relevance of language to social behaviour. He has shown that language acts to shape ways of thinking and feeling and has argued that an understanding of how it is used by different groups provides a way of understanding features of the social structure. Two ideas are basic to Bernstein's work: (1) that language and perception are intimately related and (2) that language is one of the most important means of initiating, synthesising and reinforcing ways of thinking, feeling and behaviour. He suggests that distinctive social-class languages reflect distinctive class differences in ways of thinking. Two kinds of speech system are distinguished. In lower working-class families the child learns a restricted speech system which is appropriate to his natural environment but not for his relationships with middle-class institutions, for example, schools and social agencies.

The restricted speech system, compared with the elaborated speech system of the middle class, is characterised by a reduction in adjectives and adverbs especially those which qualify feelings, and by an organisation of speech which is relatively simple, with little use of the pronoun "I" and greater use of other personal pronouns. The restricted speech system is generated by certain kinds of social relationships characterised by common assumptions, shared interests, and strong identification, which reduces the need for an individual to elaborate his intention verbally and to make it explicit. Such a speech system where feelings are taken for granted is not necessarily class linked but operates whenever social relationships are close, for example, between friends and peer groups, and in closed communities such as prisons. The restricted speech system is available to, and used by, all members of society but members of the lower working class are limited to it and have no other.

The restricted system cannot be used to communicate unique experiences which emphasise separateness and difference. It is concerned with expressing common interests and motivations and not individual motivation. Uniqueness is expressed non-verbally rather than verbally. The restricted system does not permit the individual to discriminate shades of meaning in the feelings and motivations of himself and others. This lack of perceptual discrimination is shown in the characteristic ways in which middle- and working-class parents exert authority over their children, the former tending to make person-oriented appeals and emphasising rational discussion of the consequences of actions and the feelings of other people, the latter tending to make status-oriented appeals impersonally and usually quickly followed by punishment if not obeyed.

These different attitudes to authority suggest that there are different ways of dealing with anxiety in the different social groups. Characteristic ways of dealing with anxiety in the working-class culture for the person with a restricted code involve "acting out" rather than "talking out" problems. Tensions are less subject to verbal control and tend to be dissipated quickly through action. The defence mechanisms employed are denial and displacement rather than rationalisation, which tends to be used by the middle-class person able to employ the elaborated code. An important correlate of the restricted code is that a person feels shame (that is responsibility to the group) rather than guilt (which involves the internalisation of values). Middle-class parents tend to respond in terms of the child's intent, whereas working-class parents respond in terms of the immediate consequence of the act itself and there is little verbal investigation of motive and discipline.

8. *Language, social class and social work*

Irvine (1964) suggested that in working with certain immature clients the social worker needed to use authority, give advice and set limits. In this approach the essential process consisted of an acting out of a parent–child relationship between client and social worker. However, the client's expectations as to the behaviour appropriate to a parental relationship will depend in part upon his social class. The social worker's and the client's expectations of the parental role may not coincide not because of the client's psycho-pathology but because of the conflict between their cultural definitions of the parent–child relationship.

Leonard (1966) has reviewed studies of class differences in parental roles. In middle-class families relationships tend to be more equalitarian; parental roles are less differentiated and rigidly defined. In middle-class families the father is seen as a support to the mother and as a companion to his children as well as an authority figure. In the working-class family the father often remains a rather punitive figure. The lower the social class the more rigid and punitive the father. Leonard (1968) said that it would be surprising if these culturally determined expectations were not reflected in the attitude of the client to the social worker, as a parental figure. Differences in the exercise of authority in the family reflect different patterns of expectations and values. Thus there is a need for social workers to be aware of the different expectations they may have from their clients as to what is appropriate parental behaviour. The client who uses a restricted code is likely to view the social worker as an authority figure; in some cases it may be appropriate for the social worker to use this authority directly. In other cases the social worker may need to recognise how the client regards his status although the response may not involve direction or advice.

Nursten (1965) has discussed possible implications of Bernstein's work for social work practice. It can be assumed that social workers have access to both restricted and elaborated codes. A re-examination of social work methods with lower working-class clients was required. The social worker could reinforce the use of the restricted code or could try to help the client change his code and therefore his behaviour. In long-term cases the social worker could attempt to educate clients in the use of the elaborate code. People using the restricted code may at times give powerful descriptions of their feelings through simile and metaphor. But communication problems can arise when clients are unable to express themselves in this way, and are then restricted to acting out. As we have seen for people with a restricted speech system emotional tensions are less subject to verbal control and will tend to be dissipated quickly through action. Their defence mechanisms are likely to be denial and displacement rather than rationalisation.

If the social worker recognises the client's use of the restricted code this leads to the understanding that (a) the consequences of behaviour are important to the client, (b) the social worker is viewed in terms of status as an authority figure by the client and (c) the introduction of the elaborate code would have implications for the client's defences. The social worker could help the client to develop the elaborate code by focusing on (a) the ability to abstract in general terms from a concrete situation, (b) the ability to plan ahead, (c) the ability to exercise self-control and (d) the ability to perceive the world as an ordered universe in which rational action is rewarded.

9. *Conclusion*

In concluding this chapter it may be helpful to summarise briefly some of the main points.

Patterns of interaction and methods of communication in small groups are complex and not easily understood. Social workers involved in helping in situations where there are problems of interaction between group members have to make decisions about influencing and modifying communication patterns. In trying to focus help the social worker has to decide whether to concentrate on the problems of individual members or on relationships between members, and in all cases he has to take account of the stability of the group and how it changes. The social worker needs to be clear about the functions and roles of family members and how they interrelate. Types of family may be classified according to tasks or responsibilities. Role relationships depend on the previous personality development of individuals, the demands made by group members and other people, and changes in the family or group tasks as they develop. Role complementarity may break down. The social worker is also curious about the needs and problems of family members and how these affect their relationships with others, and about lack of equilibrium.

Communication occurs on different levels. Lack of equilibrium or precarious equilibrium may be related to styles of communication which have the effect of containing the anxiety of some members while leading to blurring of roles and confusion of identity for another member. The process of socialisation involves the transmission of information about cultural expectations and requirements. Verbal language plays an important part in this process. Different patterns of child rearing and differences in the use of language in different social classes have been studied. Patterns of communication in families and between clients and social workers have to be understood both in dynamic psychological and in cultural terms. Failures in communication between clients and social workers may be due to unrecognised differences in cultural assumptions.

CHAPTER 5

Communication and the Helping Process

THIS chapter begins with two case extracts from the paper by Nursten (1965). They illustrate the points which are summarised in the previous chapter, and indicate some implications of Bernstein's work for social-work practice. They are followed by a further case study (Mrs. Blake) which also discusses these implications, but in a less detailed way. These case illustrations lead to a discussion of linguistic and intellectual development as keys to social development. The possible application of this area of theoretical and empirical work in social-work practice is then illustrated by another brief case illustration. The aim is to provide a tentative exploration of this area of research and its possible application. The tentative nature of this discussion must be emphasised. We lack experience in social work in applying some of these ideas systematically; my aim is only to suggest questions which I believe have important implications for practice.

1. *Case summary: Denise*

Denise is aged 14 and due to leave her children's home. In view of the problems before Denise's committal and during the holidays the social worker is doubtful whether Denise should return home. The social worker questions the parents and appears to want them to come to the conclusion themselves that they are unsuitable. This approach is too devious for people operating with a restricted code. A question about the holidays shows that the parents at the time had been unaware that Denise had run off for three days. Father said "If I hadn't been working I'd've known. I didn't even know she'd gone for three days. I was

working see when she went off I didn't know anything about it." Mother
said "I didn't know either.   She came in and asked for her clothes but
I said No and she went away.   I thought she was with her dad."   The
parents then quarrel in the interview about the hours of father's work
and whether or not he had ever hit Denise.   Mother ends by returning
to the theme: "She went off.   If we'd known anything about it we
wouldn't have let her go."

   The social worker goes on to ask if they really are going to apply to
have the Fit-person Order revoked.   Mother and Father replied that they
had been told to do this by the N.S.P.C.C. inspector and the Child-care
officer.   The social worker presses on and faces the father with the fact
that there is the allegation that he has interfered with Denise.   He denies
this without apparent anxiety which is again displaced and revealed by
an argument with his wife about the time a party broke up.   Father said
"Nothing happened like that.   I can honestly say nothing happened.
I'm not soft.   I could be sent to prison for that."   The social worker ends
by saying that although Denise has just got a letter from them why had
they not written to Denise for six months?   The parents looked blankly
at each other.   Mother said: "I don't know; I never thought.   I just
didn't bother writing but then I saw a letter she wrote to her Gran.   She
said she was lonely.   No one was writing to her and it was pathetic.   So
I said I'd better write."

   This excerpt is taken from Nursten's paper (1965) to which reference
has already been made.   It illustrates several points.   First, it shows certain
characteristic ways of dealing with anxiety for the person with a restricted
code (and who is without access to the elaborated code).   The mother
and father employ denial and displacement and use these defences rather
than rationalisation.   For example, they deny awareness of Denise's
behaviour and they appear not to blame or question themselves when
Denise had run off for three days.   There is no verbal explanation of why
Denise asked for her clothes.   Mother just said "No" and Denise went
away.   This also illustrates a status-oriented injunction.   There is no
discussion of what Denise was planning to do or what her motives were.
The social worker and the parents have difficulty in "understanding"
each other.   The social worker seems to want the parents to see for themselves that they are not suitable to have Denise home, and therefore to

decide not to have her. But it might have been more helpful if the social worker, recognising that she was viewed as an authority figure by the clients here, had used this authority. The social worker could have said that in her opinion she was doubtful whether Denise should return home at that time, and given reasons for the opinion. The social worker seems to have put the parents more on the defensive by discussing the alleged sexual interference and by asking why they had not written for six months. The interview might have been more free of conflict or hostility if the social worker had tried to focus on the consequences of actions, and to help the parents to relate causes and their effects or possible effects. This could have been done in constructive ways, for example, by emphasising how pleased Denise was to receive letters from her parents, or by trying to explore future plans for their daughter.

The case of Denise illustrates our earlier discussion of the possibility that communication problems may arise for people with only a restricted speech system. Such people are unable to express some feelings except by acting out; emotional tensions are less subject to verbal control. This control depends on the development of the use of the elaborated code. Commenting on the interview with Denise's parents Nursten writes: "The social worker has a conscious choice: should the restricted code be reinforced or should casework be used as an educational experience to help the client change his code and therefore his behaviour? Or should both methods be drawn on at appropriate times in dealing with the same client? In the case example *neither* is used . . . the casework process could have been different if it had been based on an understanding of communication (speech systems) and its effect on behaviour." The next case example, Tom, shows how he and his father were introduced to the use of the elaborated code through reasoning about the possible causes and results of actions.

2. *Case summary: Tom*

Father had been severely burned in an accident six years previously and his employment since had been irregular. Mother is at home (but is not referred to in the excerpts which follow). Tom is 16, suffers from epilepsy and has been in a psychiatric hospital because of a ?psychotic episode. He has been aggressive and has threatened his siblings with a knife, and he has run away from home. Casework has been geared to helping the parents to set limits and to helping Tom build controls, see the consequences of his behaviour, and talk out rather than act out by the introduction of an elaborate code.

I told Tom that I was concerned about his carrying a knife because it might mean trouble if he got into a situation where he felt he had to use it. If he were carrying it to protect himself he might sometimes feel he had to protect himself by using it. Tom said disgustedly that he did not carry it for protection; he needed it sometimes in school, to cut string or something. Tom asked: "Is it so unusual to carry a knife?" I told him that it wasn't unusual at all. I wondered if the boys at school knew he carried the knife. He thought so. "Do they know you've been in hospital?" He did not know: he has told one boy but thinks the kids would have teased him about it by now if they knew about it. I suggested we put ourselves in other people's shoes for a minute and see how it seemed to them to have a classmate who (1) was bigger than most of the boys in the class, (2) had been in a hospital and (3) was carrying a knife. "How do you think they feel?" Tom was amazed. "Do you mean they are afraid of me?" "That's a possibility; maybe they feel they need to carry knives for their protection too." "You make me sound as though I were going to knife somebody at any minute." Tom said this with hostility. We continued talking about the knife. "O.K. so I won't carry a knife any more. Can I ask you something if we are through with that?" We went on to other things, one of them being how angry he'd got at his sister when she'd told him to shut up. His response was to jump on her hair curler, breaking it. I wondered if this were an immediate reaction or whether he had thought about it. Immediate. I commented that this was why I worried about his carrying a knife; if he got cornered, he might use it without stopping to think. "I might use it if the other boy were coming at me with a knife." I thought that if he did not have a knife the other boy would not have to draw his. I think he could see the point of this. I said it was his decision—carrying a knife. There wasn't too much anyone could do if he really was determined to do something. However, he should realise the risks he was taking.

I went over these risks versus his goal of staying at home. I told him that if the pleasure was worth the risk of getting into trouble and maybe getting sent to hospital, then he would go ahead anyway, but he should think about this before he decided. The interview ended with Tom asking what was I going to do with the knife? Keep it? I said "No, he could have it back." Then he said I could keep it until next week. Tom finally decided he would keep the knife, saying he would not carry it to school.

In a subsequent interview with Tom's father, in discussing what it was that prevented most children from attacking parents, father guessed that the child loses all desire to hit his parents. I add: "Or learns that he can't get away with it." I wondered if it were just coincidence that Tom had started to act out just around the time when father had been burned so badly and was actually weaker than Tom, unable to do much about enforcing any controls. Father said, in a tone of revelation, that the first time he could remember Tom having a temper outburst was one day during this period.

The social worker here begins by stating her own concern about Tom carrying a knife. This is stated clearly and is linked with what it could mean, i.e. what the consequences could be. Tom's denial that he does not carry the knife for protection is not challenged: in fact, the social worker agrees that carrying a knife, in itself, is not unusual. The conversation proceeds, apparently in a fairly relaxed way, and the social worker is able to suggest looking at things from other people's points of view. In this way Tom is helped to look at his own behaviour and role(s) in a more detached way and is encouraged to generalise on the basis of the preceding talk about his action in carrying the knife. He decides not to carry the knife any more and then discusses the future. The social worker encourages him to think about exercising self-control by pointing out that he should realise the risks he was taking. He carried responsibility for his decisions but the making of decisions involves looking at sequences of actions. In his case one sequence runs from the carrying of a knife by someone who acts very impulsively sometimes, to the use of a knife. A second sequence runs from not carrying a knife to not being able to use a knife, and not having to face the consequences of using it against, or provoking, another person.

Their joint review of Tom's situation and their looking ahead involves the social worker and Tom in ordering ideas in a cooler and more objective manner than happened in the case of Denise's parents. Tom is encouraged to look at the possibilities of rational, planned action which involves him in exercising, or trying to exercise, control of his impulses. Tom's father is helped to see that changed circumstances brought changed behaviour. Again, cause and effect are related.

The reader will observe that in both of the cases quoted so far, Denise and Tom, the social workers were assertive: they deliberately directed attention to certain subjects and gave clear indications of their own ideas about aspects of behaviour. In particular they were concerned about their clients' capacity for self-direction and self-control. We have noted how in some cases it may be appropriate for the social worker to use authority directly in this way. In other cases, as in the interview with Denise's parents, certain kinds of assertiveness may be inappropriate. The social worker's behaviour in that interview appears to reflect to some extent the influence of psycho-analytic ideas on the profession. To assess them critically is not to denigrate the value of the contribution. These ideas led to stress being placed on the concept of client self-determination and to the idea that a person might not be entirely responsible for his condition but should, nevertheless, be expected to assume responsibility for his own behaviour. Social workers have therefore tried to help their clients to exercise choice and accept responsibility for making their own decisions. They have adopted non-directive techniques. The caseworker seemed to be trying to do these things with Denise's parents. She tried to allow their self-determination at one level. She was also set on the clients' seeing and saying that they were not suitable to have Denise with them. The earlier discussion gives reasons for saying that these aims were inappropriate. Non-directive techniques can be and, of course, are, used where clients have the motivation and capacity to respond to them. But authority too can be used constructively, in the best interests of clients. Of course, there is nothing new in this idea. But we are becoming gradually more able to differentiate situations where it may and may not be used constructively, and some of the social and psychological influences on peoples' perception of authority. For example, Leonard's (1966) review of class differences in the perception of parental roles was mentioned in the previous chapter. Further reference will be made to social workers' and clients' expectations of the parental relationship and how these may diverge for other reasons than the client's psychopathology. Cultural definitions of the parent–child relationship have to be borne in mind.

These questions of assertiveness, the appropriate use of authority and the development of verbal controls are all raised by the further case examples in this chapter. In the first case, Mrs. Blake, it seems that it was fully appropriate to use material aid and other forms of practical help and that these were ways in which the social worker communicated concern. Later, Mrs. Blake discovered that there were things she could do for herself which before she might have hoped other people would do for her. In the case of Mr. Brown, the probation officer helped his client to identify his own areas of responsibility gradually. As these became clearer through discussion with his probation officer, Mr. Brown seemed to become more confident in dealing with them. For example, he recognised that his decision to avoid contact with the police and to keep out of trouble involved not becoming involved with gangs of teenagers, and not infringing laws relating to motor cycles. First, however, I introduce Mrs. Blake. This will be followed by discussion of some aspects of language and social development.

3. *Case summary: Mrs. Blake*

Mr. Blake had left his wife and was living with his mother in a nearby town. The family was known to a number of social agencies and had been discussed by members of a standing case conference for several years. There was a long history of rent arrears. It was said that Mr. and Mrs. Blake neglected their council house and did not care properly for their children. A N.S.P.C.C. inspector, Education Welfare officer, and a Health Department Welfare officer had visited the family for several years. Mrs. Abell, the Child-care officer, became actively involved when it was reported at the case conference that the rent arrears were again high and that the Housing Department proposed to evict Mrs. Blake and the children.

When Mrs. Abell first visited the home, Mrs. Blake was suspicious and unwelcoming. The early interviews took place on the doorstep. Mrs. Blake said that she had difficulty in managing financially and Mrs. Abell offered her some clothes for the children. Mrs. Blake accepted the offer. When Mrs. Abell called to give her the clothes Mrs. Blake was still on her guard but invited the Child-care officer into the house. When Mrs. Abell reviewed the case some time later she commented that initially contact was difficult because so many social workers had visited the family previously and some had offered little other than criticism.

Mrs. Blake paid the rent arrears and after providing the clothes Mrs. Abell did not visit again for three months. Then she received a message from the Education Welfare officer. The children's teachers thought that they were being neglected. Mrs. Abell took some more clothes for the children and Mrs. Blake again invited her to enter the house. She still seemed suspicious of Mrs. Abell who learned that other workers had threatened to have the children removed as a way of inducing Mrs. Blake to "improve her care of them". Mrs. Abell reassured the mother that she did not wish to remove the children. Mrs. Blake's mother had also accused her of neglecting the children. It seemed to Mrs. Abell that her client had had so much adverse criticism that she had lost hope and self-respect and felt unable to cope any better. At this point Mrs. Blake felt more able to discuss her situation with the Child-care officer and told her about the marital difficulties and financial problems. Mrs. Abell took Mrs. Blake to see the Housing manager and an official of the Ministry of Social Security. It was agreed that the Ministry would make direct payments to the Housing Department for the rent. It seemed that Mrs. Blake appreciated Mrs. Abell's support in these two interviews and was a little more hopeful.

Shortly after this Mrs. Blake was admitted to hospital urgently. A relative cared for the children. In hospital Mrs. Blake met another of Mrs. Abell's clients whose approving comments about the Child-care officer seemed to help Mrs. Blake feel less resentful. While she was in hospital the Education Welfare officer, N.S.P.C.C. inspector and the Health visitor visited Mrs. Blake's home. Mrs. Abell contacted them about the situation.

After her recovery Mrs. Blake proudly showed Mrs. Abell some interior decorating she had done. During the visit she said she would like to be reconciled to her husband. Mrs. Abell took her client to the Children's Department office for a meeting with Mr. Blake but following this it seemed an immediate reconciliation was unlikely.

In later visits Mrs. Abell found her client to be relaxed and friendly, accepting offers of practical help, for example, in purchasing decorating materials with money provided by the Children's Department. The Housing Department did not proceed with the eviction, although the rent again fell into arrears and the client and the Child-care officer were interviewed again by the Housing manager.

After interviews with Mr. and Mrs. Blake separately and further discussions with the Housing manager, the couple were reunited and moved to a different council house. The marital situation continued to be unstable and several times Mrs. Blake discussed the possibility of leaving her husband. She did not do so. It seemed that through talking with Mrs. Abell she was able to examine impulsive decisions and to revise them. Mrs. Abell thought that if the family were to remain together long then further help would be required. The children did receive affection but Mrs. Blake had little idea about how to control them. But they did have a sense of belonging to a family and if Mrs. Blake left her husband she would face difficult problems of accommodation and the risk of further family breakdown.

Mrs. Abell had to liaise with a number of other workers during the nine months covered by this summary. There were considerable difficulties for the Child-care officer in working with some other staff whose perceptions of the situation were sometimes remarkably different from hers. The Health visitor and general practitioner in particular were unwilling to help Mrs. Blake and both refused to visit her at home when the Child-care officer asked for their help.

Barriers to communication between client and social worker are noted at the beginning of the summary. At first Mrs. Blake did not see Mrs. Abell as a potentially helpful person but rather as an unhelpful authority figure. In the past, some social workers who had had dealings with the family had offered little other than unconstructive criticism. At the beginning Mrs. Blake tended to deny that she had difficulties. Later she acknowledges these and is able to accept clothes for the children.

The Child-care officer's actions in providing material and practical help were a tangible way of expressing interest and concern. They also seemed to convey recognition of the difficulties, and to indicate that these could be approached in certain ways with satisfactory results. The client was able to learn ways of coping by seeing how the Child-care officer coped. Members of the family found it difficult to express themselves verbally because of limited vocabulary which, although adequate for familiar situations, may have been insufficient to enable them to express their feelings. They seemed to find it difficult to follow through a process of reasoning and to structure their ideas about their experience. The inability to express and to discuss ideas about experience hinders the capacity for adaptation.

The main work with the family took place in the home. In the home visit the social worker can use a number of different avenues of communication and may sometimes arrive or be called in at a crisis point (Levine, 1965). Mrs. Abell commented that real contact was established only after she had helped over a crisis and had been seen to support Mrs. Blake in dealing with other agencies. Mrs. Abell used different forms of verbal and non-verbal behaviour in effecting some changes both in the situation and in the client's behaviour.

Mrs. Abell did not employ a form of language useful for discussing shades of feeling and motives and involving comprehension of intentions at too early a stage in the contact. The use of the elaborated code would probably have led to greater defensiveness and passivity on the part of the client. Mrs. Blake was encouraged to be active and she became less defensive as her relationship with the worker developed. At a later stage more sophisticated language was used in discussing the marital difficulties. Mrs. Blake was then able to make use of the discussion in deciding on a course of action, for example, staying with her husband.

4. *Communication and cognitive and emotional development*

Although the social implications must be kept foremost in understanding language and other forms of communication, it is important to recognise that the possession of language offers advantages to the individual in addition to those it offers to him as a member of a group. A child learns his language in a social situation and for social reasons, but once he has learned it his orientation towards himself and his problems is altered.

Pavlov was concerned with how the mass of information or stimuli from the external world signals its properties to the organism. He recognised that the ability to speak enlarged a person's potentialities. His theory was that for men words act as stimuli, but not simply as dogs react to verbal commands. He described the conditioned reflex mechanisms that all animals share as the first signal system. Verbal stimuli formed a second signal system. He said that in the animal reality is signalised almost exclusively by stimulations and the traces they make in the brain and receptors. Men also possess this in the shape of impressions, sensations and ideas of the world around them, with the exception of oral and written speech. This is the first signal system. Speech constitutes a second system of signals of reality which is a signal of the first signals. The second signal system is peculiar to human beings. The fundamental laws governing the activity of the first signalling system also govern the second signal system (Hilgard and Bower, 1966).

Piaget proposed a framework for studying stages in the child's development of ways of adapting to the world. As children grow they become increasingly capable of recognising relationships between data in a given situation. This growing ability is due not only to the accumulation of experience of the perception of objects but also to the use of language in symbolising the data.

Piaget described the first two years of life as the presymbolic sensorimotor stage of behaviour. After this the child begins to internalise symbols and enters the pre-operational stage which continues until about the age of 7. At this stage the child can use symbols in dealing with a familiar situation. But his behaviour remains pre-operational so long as he cannot use symbols as a means of relating a new situation to past situations. He advances to this stage of concrete operations, normally after the age of 7, when he is able to deal with the new situation by consciously assimilating to it his past experiences and adapting these to the new situation. To do this he needs to conceptualise and for this numerical and verbal symbols are necessary. The child needs to be able to carry forward his earlier schema and to modify it in transfer to the new situation.

In other words, to deal with a new situation the child has to exercise skill in dealing with a mixture of the familiar and unfamiliar. He must bring the past up to the present (remember) and he must project himself beyond his present experience (imagine). There is no hard and fast division between these two forms of mental behaviour. The processes by which recall of the past is accomplished are those used in anticipating the future. In remembering a person builds a schema. In imagining he freely builds events together that go to the making of several different schemata. In studying children's (and adult's) behaviour it is apparent that what has been learned previously tends to persist and change is resisted. The effects of a past situation may be carried forward into the present without verbal symbolisation. The past persists strongly in children's behaviour. If there is symbolisation by language there are two possible effects. By enabling him to symbolise the past language re-inforces a child's conservation of past experience. By enabling the child to keep the past situation in his mind he may be helped to bring it more into relation with the new situation. Language is important when the child needs to deal with causal relationships. The symbolisation may be non-verbal, but carrying a picture of cause and effect relationships may be too restrictive and too closely connected with particular events to be generally useful. Language is needed if the child is to be free to explore new combinations of relationships (Piaget, 1952).

Intellectual growth depends upon the emergence of two forms of competence. As they grow children (a) acquire ways of representing recurrent regularities in their environment and (b) transcend the momentary by linking past to present to future. They develop ways of (a) representation and (b) integration. Most of the necessary innovations are transmitted to the child by other members of his culture. He learns ways of responding, looking and imagining and ways of translating what he has encountered into language. Vehicles of representation which successively emerge are actions, images and words.

The child develops skill in representing the environment to himself in three stages. First, past events are represented through appropriate motor responses, for example, holding a cup to the mouth (orectic representation). Second, the child builds up a mental image of a situation, formed from a number of images of similar situations. Little is known about how these images are formed (iconic representation). This stage shades gradually into the next (symbolic representation) when, in children between the ages of 4 and 12, language comes to play an increasingly important role as a means of knowing. It shapes arguments and even supersedes the child's earlier ways of processing information. When experience can be translated into symbolic form it is possible to achieve remote reference, transformation and combination of ideas (Bruner, 1964).

Two features of language are remoteness and arbitrariness. It permits productive combinations of cognitive operations in the absence of what is represented. With this achievement the child can delay gratification by representing to himself what lies beyond the present, and what other possibilities exist beyond the clue that is under his role. The child may be ready for delay of gratification. Language helps him to accomplish this.

5. *Language and social adaptation*

Vygotsky (1962) and Luria and Yudovitch (1968) regard linguistic and intellectual development as keys to social development. By naming objects and defining their connections and relations the adult creates new forms of reflection of reality in the child more complex than those which he could have formed through individual experience. This process of the transmission of information and the formation of concepts which is the basic way the adult influences the child, constitutes the central process of the child's intellectual development.

As the child learns to subordinate himself to language it begins to act as a regulator of behaviour and to give him new forms of attention, memory, imagination, thought and action. At first the child is physically controlled by the adult. Later, the adult is able to control the child's activity by verbal means. This development is gradual. Speech at first has only an impelling function, acting almost as a signal and nothing else. Once an instruction is given the child acts on it but may ignore further instructions. At a later stage the semantic aspect of speech becomes decisive; the child attends to the meaning of words and regulates his activity according to their meaning. Speech becomes internalised and the child no longer needs the reinforcement provided by his own words. This, of course, is the prototype of adult self-regulation. Under stress a person may revert to the earlier form of regulating behaviour by talking to himself or telling himself what to do.

The symbolising and conceptual nature of language modify conditioning processes and introduce a new flexibility into the child's activities. Language makes possible the setting up of generalised classes of responses. Once a stimulus is seen to belong to a recognisable class of stimuli it will immediately lead to the response appropriate to that class. Language also makes possible planned behaviour in which the child formulates aims of his behaviour, and plans for achieving these aims.

Language use is the means by which many environmental influences are synthesised and reinforced. Spoken language powerfully conditions what the child learns and how he learns and thus influences future learning.

Language also makes a progressive contribution to the child's awareness of himself. It relates him as an individual to other people. It helps to transmit group values and norms of behaviour to him and thus influences his attitudes (Bernstein, 1961).

In studying the overall course of the child's development it appears that language has a constant and comprehensive effect on cognitive growth (perception, remembering, imagining, conceiving, judging and reasoning), and emotional development. Where a child's hearing is impaired or where life in an institution is not conducive to easy and constant intercourse between a child and adults, to take two examples, linguistic development is impeded and cognitive and emotional development is retarded.

For a child's speech to become a means of communication his cognitive powers must be exercised. At the same time there needs to be frequent opportunity for communication. The transformation of the child's attempts to speak into a means of communication and of symbolising his own behaviour depends to a great degree on the response of others to him. It is here that the handicap of deaf children or those in institutions may be most severe. Where the pattern of everyday life is a routine in which the child's recurrent needs are consistently and regularly met there is little need for the child to verbalise his demands. If at other times adults are unable to attend to him and fail to respond to what he says the child's progress in linguistic development is likely to be slow. Cognitive and emotional immaturity follow.

One of the most dramatic examples of environmental influence on language behaviour and development is institutionalisation. Studies of institutionalised children indicate that social factors, even at a very early age, have a significant and possibly permanent influence on linguistic and intellectual development (Bowlby, 1965).

6. *Language deficiency, social maladjustment and social-work practice*

Deficient language development may thus cause difficulty in the mastery of more complex systems of thought and in the control of behaviour. It may also affect a person's self-image and capacity for self-awareness. Inadequate stimulation of a child by illiterate or semi-literate parents is an important factor in class differences in ability and achievement. Linguistic disability impairs a person's ability to cope effectively with his environment. The physical and psychological effects interact and are mutually reinforcing. Cultural deprivation occurs in families where parents are preoccupied with their own activities and neglect their children.

These generalisations are supported by the results of attempts to help children in these kinds of situations. At first children progress most noticeably in their emotional uses of language and in their social behaviour. Later progress is observed in cognitive ability as measured by verbal tests of intelligence. It seems likely that as the child responds to warmer personal care and attention his social behaviour improves. His language develops and this promotes effectiveness and precision in his perception and conceptual thinking and fosters greater discrimination in, and awareness of, social attitudes (Lewis, 1963).

The role of verbal and non-verbal learning in social adaptation and problem solving has important implications for social-work practice. Clients can be effectively helped to analyse their situations verbally and through other forms of communication with social workers. In this

F

way new perspectives could result from new forms of perception. Such learning occurs gradually, ways of dealing with a problem being worked out slowly and laboriously. It may also occur suddenly, the client becoming more aware of logical connections and new ways of interpreting and coping with difficulties.

Jehu (1967), Picardie (1967) and Holder (1969) have discussed processes involved in adaptive changes in the behaviour of clients either in direct treatment with a social worker or indirectly through changes in the client's environment which were promoted by a social worker. The reduction of environmental stress may be achieved in ways which strengthen a client's adaptive behaviour. The stressful behaviour of people in the client's environment may be modified by similar techniques.

The case summary which follows illustrates some of these points. It shows how a probation officer identified his client's difficulties in communication and found ways of helping.

7. *Case summary: Mr. Brown*

Mr. Brown, aged 24, was placed under supervision after pleading not guilty to an indecent assault on a girl who had denied in court that the incident had occurred. Other evidence against him was fairly conclusive. Mr. Green, the probation officer, found that his client was virtually a non-reader and writer when he left school, was of low intelligence, dependent on others and easily led. He was slow in thought and speech. About the offence, he maintained that he had only kissed and cuddled the girl and had not known that this was wrong. He had been thoroughly frightened by the court appearance. The probation officer thought that Mr. Brown would find it helpful to talk about his situation to an adult outside his family. It seemed that the client's difficulties in social adaptation, not only in his relationships with girls, were partly due to his low intelligence and his home circumstances were unlikely to help him come to terms with them to any great extent. Mr. Brown seemed to be emotionally insecure and lonely. The problems perceived by Mr. Green were of rather a general nature. From the client's point of view his problem was to avoid further contact with the police. He did not understand what "all the fuss" had been about.

At first Mr. Brown seemed extremely slow and deliberately on his guard in the interviews with the probation officer. A turning point came when Mr. Green showed ignorance about his client's work. Mr. Brown derived obvious satisfaction in explaining it to the probation officer. It seemed to give him satisfaction to feel that he was competent in an area where Mr. Green was clearly far from infallible. The probation officer asserted his authority later in the interview through discussion of the requirements of probation. This pattern was repeated in later interviews, the client being encouraged to assert himself, while Mr. Green showed that he too could be assertive while remaining friendly.

As the relationship developed Mr. Brown found it easier to put his thoughts into words and to discuss his ideas with Mr. Green. He appreciated having a good listener. Although his limited intellectual ability was a handicap, his self-confidence seemed to develop and his verbal capacity increased although, to quote Mr. Green, "this did not run to the art of being indignant or angry in words."

A further significant development occurred about seven months after the order was made. Mr. Brown told the probation officer about one of his friends who changed jobs frequently. He was critical of this and said it was time his friend settled down. The way in which Mr. Brown discussed this seemed to indicate a marked improvement in his capacity for self-expression and reasoning. Seven months earlier the client would not have been able to think about the behaviour of another person, or about his own behaviour, in this way. By this time he felt able to talk quite freely to the probation officer. He now seemed to have a number of friends whereas at the beginning of his contact with Mr. Green he had been lonely. He responded to the probation officer's encouragement to take more interest in his personal appearance.

The early definition of roles in this case appeared to be important to the client who, it seems, quickly gained confidence in the probation officer as someone who respected him and was willing to learn from him, as well as being someone who could be firm in exercising authority. It seemed that Mr. Green encouraged his client to think for himself about this definition of roles. He tried to help his client to feel less anxious about their relationship, at the same time encouraging him to discuss his situation. This encouragement was given in ways which were not too emotionally threatening to Mr. Brown. The probation officer did this by using simple language and by repeating what he had said until Mr. Brown indicated that he had grasped what the words were intended to convey.

The way in which Mr. Green behaved in listening and responding to his client tended to reinforce certain behaviour. Mr. Green's initiatives and responses appeared to be aimed at helping the client to organise his thoughts through verbal discussion. It seemed that as Mr. Brown's communicative capacity improved he seemed to develop in his cognitive abilities. His ability to generalise and conceptualise seemed to improve. He developed a greater capacity for self-direction and self-control. His confidence and self-esteem also seemed to be enhanced. It seems quite possible that improved communicative capacity contributed significantly to Mr. Brown's capacity to cope with his situation and to his social adaptation.

CHAPTER 6

The Social Agency and the Social Worker

1. Organisation and communication

Administrative organisation may be said to consist of a set of people collaborating and communicating with each other in a systematic and continuing fashion for the performance of a common task. Different tasks call different patterns of collaboration into being. Since one person may play a part in several tasks he may be a member of several "organisations". Organisation is thus a term which is used to describe certain kinds of human co-operation. The structure of organisation and the administrative process cannot be described without reference to specific tasks. An organisation thus consists of more or less specialised roles played by people in dealing with a task, and the pattern of communication and co-operation which links them together.

The purpose of administration is to link the people who provide or control resources, the people who perform the tasks that convert these resources into goods or services and those who use the products or outcome of this work. If these three groups are not effectively and continuously linked, the work cannot be done. The co-ordinating relationships which create an organisation of individuals carrying out a task arise from the fact that these individuals do not have the time, information, power and ability to decide all their actions independently. They cannot decide everything for themselves but depend repeatedly on others for the information, guidance and instructions that enable them to do their work. The organisation determines the timing, direction and content of the communications on which they depend and many of the assumptions and aims that guide them. Each time they rely on past or present communications with someone else when making a decision they confer "power" of some kind on the person upon whom they rely.

In most organisations specific people or groups are required to make certain decisions. The individuals concerned may largely determine for themselves what should be done or they may merely approve recommendations put to them by others in the organisation. But a decision cannot strictly be said to have been taken until the designated person or group has approved it. This type of power may be called "formal authority". It should be distinguished from prestige, the general influence exercised by senior staff over juniors. Prestige may be attached to certain posts or groups in an organisation or to certain skills. It may be exercised by junior members of staff, for example, because of the character or past history of the person concerned.

The analysis of an organisation in terms of communication should not lead to the assumption that a member of staff's responses can be determined simply by the character and timing of the stimuli to which he is subjected. He has his own attitudes and ideas which dispose him to act in certain ways although these may be influenced or modified by organisations (Donnison, 1965).

The term social agency is frequently used to indicate the unit of organisation in which the social worker is employed. Such units of organisation may be referred to as departments, for example, a local authority Social Services department or a hospital Social Work department. Social agencies may thus be large or small units to which the social worker has a sense of belonging together with committee members and administrative and clerical staff. Organisations while having their own identities and structures, do not exist independently of their environment. They are created out of society and have an effect on society. Social agencies have been conceived as organisations "fashioned to express the will of a society, or of some group in that society, as to social welfare" (Perlman, 1957).

Organisation patterns frequently change. With the implementation of the Local Authority Social Services Act, 1970, new Social Services Committees in England and Wales have assumed responsibility for the functions formerly exercised by welfare and children's committees and some of the functions of health committees. Thus the Social Services departments are large organisations (compared with the former Children's departments, for example) and staff are engaged in formulating new policies and procedures. It is not yet clear what the effects of reorganisation will be on the services provided. Changes in the work of probation officers have been discussed by Parsloe (1967). The Probation and After-care officer has become more concerned with adult offenders and may now be more accurately described as a social worker for the penal system (rather than of the courts). Past experience and information about managerial methods will provide some guidelines in coping with such changes. These two concluding chapters will draw on these resources. In a sense books are often out of date by the time they reach the press but their subject matter often makes this inevitable.

A social agency, like other organisations, consists of the more or less specialised roles played by those who carry out its tasks. The social worker's role is partly defined by the objectives of the organisation which employs him. This means that the social agency makes an essential contribution to the nature of the social worker's activities. Its duties, powers, policies and methods play an important part in defining the ways in which the social worker tries to help the client. The social worker thus has an interest in modifying and developing the agency in which he works, and the services which it provides, as well as those provided by other organisations (Donnison *et al.*, 1965).

The idea of the function of the agency is of central importance for the social worker. It links the social worker and the agency with the community. The function of the agency is the meeting point of social worker and client and it gives their relationship its purpose and helps it to evolve (Timms, 1964 b).

Large organisations are composed of a number of smaller groups. It is possible to hold a primary group together in the absence of adequate face-to-face communication but there is a tendency for it to break up or subdivide after it has reached a certain critical size (on average between eight and ten people).

In the small primary group the individual members are interrelated by a network of personal relationships. Each member has a more or less clearly defined attitude towards every other member, whether the feeling is liking, disliking or indifference. The attitude of individuals to

the complex, formal organisation is likely to be determined by the extent
to which its goals coincide, or conflict with, those of their own primary
groups.   If the worker feels that the interests of his organisation clash
with those of his working group, no amount of propaganda, pleading or
discipline will lead him to develop feelings of loyalty towards the organisation. He will act in accordance with his own social norms which may not
correspond with the interests of the whole organisation. The primary
group is the instrument of society through which in large measure the
individual acquires his attitudes, opinions, goals and ideals; it is also one
of the fundamental sources of discipline and social controls. It is the
most potent influence in regulating the individual's behaviour.   In
attempting to change some aspects of human behaviour the approach
should therefore be made through the medium of the group rather than
through the individual, if success is to be likely. It is important to realise
that the informal working group is the source of social control. Legiti-
mate control should be exercised through such groups and it is said
that they should not be broken up (Brown, 1954).

2. *Organisation goals and channels of communication*

The "task" approach to the study of organisation involves analysis of
the work to be done and the techniques and resources available to do it.
Newman (1966) explains these ideas in the following way. All organisations have objectives and in many cases they have a number of objectives.
To achieve objectives work must be done. To do work resources must
be deployed and the work done is determined by the effective resources
deployed. The goals of an organisation and its members are not easily
defined and, over a period of time they often change; they may be
added to, or modified, or superseded by new goals. At a given point in
time the goals may be simple or complex, they may be compatible or
conflicting, and they may be interpreted differently, by different members
of the organisation. In multi-purpose organisations conflicts between
goals are likely to occur when the different goals make incompatible

demands on the organisation. This is illustrated in discussions about the teaching and research activities of universities, for example. Another problem in considering organisational goals is that the individual members of an organisation have individual needs and it cannot be assumed that they are automatically committed to furthering the stated goals of the organisation. Different members of staff have different perceptions of objectives. Simon (1965) argued that individuals accept membership of an organisation when their activity in it contributes directly or indirectly to their own personal goals. The strategy adopted to achieve goals, and the goals themselves, are interwoven. Questions of values arise in considering both goals and alternative means to their achievement.

Etzioni (1964) points out that formal statements about the goals of an organisation may not represent the actual goals. Different members of staff may have their own versions of what the goals are. Although in some situations there may be agreement on the organisations' goals among staff, resources may be distributed in such a way that goals different from the stated goals are pursued.

Brown (1960) has suggested that an organisation can be studied from four different points of view. First, there is the manifest organisation, the situation as it is formally described and displayed. Many organisations have tasks, procedures and an organisation which can be written down or described in an organisation chart. Then there is the assumed version of the organisation, the situation as it is assumed to be by the individual concerned. The people who work in the organisation have their own interpretation of the system and this may or may not be consistent with other versions. The extant version is the situation as revealed by systematic exploration and analysis. Fourth, there is the requisite organisation. This is the version which looks to the future and it consists of opinions about the tasks, procedures, and pattern of organisation which ought to be adopted.

The formal communications system is the official hierarchy. Decisions and information are transmitted downwards and information flows upwards. But communication channels cannot be correlated exclusively with channels of authority. Communication occurs within the hierarchy, but there is also communication in the informal organisation, based on the social interaction of individuals. Thus there may be cliques of individuals, or groups who accept leadership outside the formal system. If the formal and informal aspects of an organisation are incompatible, tension obviously occurs while another possibility is open conflict. On the other hand, organisational efficiency may increase because of the friendliness and co-operation within the informal system. Thus in addition to facilitating the transmission of information and conveying instructions, communication can also serve to strengthen the bonds between individuals and the organisation. The organisation achieves its purposes through the behaviour of all its members (Warham, 1967).

An important function of a system of formal organisation is thus its definition of a network of positions linked by channels of communication. An essential correlate of the formal structure is a records system. Records are a mechanism through which the activities of individuals may be related in an orderly way to the needs and purposes of the organisation. They may also be a way of providing members of staff and other people with information about an organisation's activities (Simon, 1965).

The performance of a task depends on the evidence about the situation available to the worker, the information he is able to obtain about it, and the way in which he interprets the information. Work is based on (a) an analysis of the task to be performed, (b) the aims of the worker, (c) planning, on the basis of the facts of the situation, the interpretation of the facts and the aims perceived by the worker and (d) control and evaluation for the purpose of seeing whether and how the aims are achieved or modified.

Records are important in this process, especially when a number of people are, or may become, involved in the work. Recorded information can be helpful in co-ordinating efforts to reach agreed objectives. Records are an important means of communication between social workers in the same agency, between social workers in different agencies, and between social workers and other people such as administrators and executive committees.

The purposes of case records in social work may be summarised as (a) practice—to ensure adequate service to the client, (b) administration—to review and evaluate the discharge of responsibility, (c) teaching and supervision—to communicate knowledge and improve skill and (d) research—to discover new knowledge and to assist in social planning and prevention (Hamilton, 1946).

The form in which case records are kept is supposed to be closely related to the purposes they serve. There is no such thing as a model record but there are some common styles of recording and some common characteristics of a useful record. Narrative recording of day-to-day events as they occur ensures that information is recorded quickly and, in emergency, the current situation can be ascertained promptly provided that the record has been kept up to date. Summarised recording may take the form of either a chronological narrative, or an arrangement of the information under headings. This method is supposed to encourage the social worker to analyse and think productively about the information. The record should point to the meaning and relative importance of the information. If a record is to be a practical aid it must be readable. It should be compiled in such a way that busy people can quickly obtain from it information which they require. It should be plain, clear and brief. Brevity should reflect real understanding of what has been observed and the ability to give essential information concisely.

Social workers sometimes use a combination of methods. A common practice is to make careful summaries at intervals as a means of recapitulation and review of evidence appearing earlier in the record. These summaries indicate the social worker's assessment of the development of the case, state the aims of the work and reasons for their revision. In a useful record interpretation of the meaning of the case is as important as the reporting of the facts.

In deciding on the content of case records, reports and letters the social worker considers the purpose of the communication. This means considering (a) what the reader needs to know in order to respond, for example by taking appropriate action or providing information, (b) what other evidence may be relevant and of help to the reader and (c) what information should be recorded, bearing in mind what one is at liberty to disclose (Hamilton, 1946; Davison, 1965).

The use of written records in social work raises issues of confidentiality. It is commonly assumed that information given to social workers is used responsibly in the interests of clients and not in ways contrary to the moral obligations assumed by the social worker in his professional role.

Applying the principle of confidentiality is not always easy in practice. In working with other people, however, the social worker is helped in deciding how much information it is appropriate to share by trying to understand the roles other people may play in helping the client. The social worker has to consider how other people, such as teachers, health visitors or policemen, will use information, and what information they may need in order to carry out their tasks. Clients are usually aware that information is being given to other people and have usually given their consent to this being done.

Clarification of responsibility in using information is by no means simple. When, for example, social workers feel that they should make representations to their employers or to government about under-privileged people or about people who appear to have been unjustly treated it may be exceedingly difficult. Social workers individually or as a group may be faced by difficult moral dilemmas. Decisions about the needs of individuals and the welfare of the community raise difficult and complex issues about the availability and communication of evidence on which they may be based (Day, 1968).

3. *Communication problems in organisations*

Hostilities between individuals may be increased by some forms of social organisation. Some groups are divided in order to utilise feelings of hostility and competitiveness on the rather crude assumption that competition between groups or individuals acts as an incentive to "better" work or increased output. Workers may experience conflicting feelings and attitudes about the situation and as a result the competitive system may not work in the way intended. Such situations may breed feelings of resentment, confusion and insecurity and workers may become suspicious of the system as well as each other.

For example, a large psychiatric hospital was reorganised in small self-contained units for some clinical purposes. Each unit had its own doctors, nurses and social worker. A senior psychiatric social worker was appointed and asked to co-ordinate the social work in the hospital as a whole. The senior psychiatric social worker tried to encourage regular meetings of the social workers. One social worker of long experience decided from the start not to attend these meetings although, alone among the social workers, she was able to express her resentment directly about the senior's appointment and to support the senior psychiatric social worker in other ways. The social workers were suspicious of the senior P.S.W.'s role and resented his appointment. There were diffuse expressions of hostility at the meetings and sometimes members would not come, or would leave the meetings prematurely. Other members of the hospital staff seemed to feel threatened by the meetings, and inquired about the discussions. One social worker was asked by a unit doctor not to discuss her cases at the meetings. Initially the attempt was to discuss topics which the social workers felt concerned about, for example, the question of confidentiality, the keeping of records and so on. Comparisons of the nature of the work done in different units and differences in methods of work provided a later focus. The group learned, for example, about the different kinds of referrals they received. There were fairly wide variations in the nature of referrals which reflected varying degrees of interest in social work, and understanding of it, among the doctors. The social workers tended to look to the doctors for advice about how to do their work and their insecurity was enhanced if the doctors were unable or unwilling to give this.

The social workers experienced conflict between their attendance at the meetings and their unit loyalties, finding it hard to reconcile the latter with the idea of co-operation with colleagues. After a time the meetings led to some sharing of information and they appeared to provide some mutual support. The possible advantages of co-ordination might have been appreciated to some extent, and feelings of rivalry and suspicion could be expressed directly. But the possibility of co-operative action seemed to be directly at variance with the way in which staff perceived the unit system.

The meetings were not entirely successful and were finally abandoned, since it was clear that the social workers would resist attempts to co-ordinate social work in the hospital, and they would not accept the leadership of the senior P.S.W. It seemed that the meetings were almost bound to terminate because of the conflict between the social workers' assumptions about the unit system and what would be involved in co-operative effort. In other ways the meetings had limited success. They led to some slight modification of the feelings of distance, suspicion and rivalry and they provided the possibility of more direct expressions of hostility. Previously, the social workers did not have a single focus for their hostility and their feelings of frustration accumulated. In such situations workers tend to forget the original reasons for their sense of grievance, blaming "them" or finding other people against whom to feel resentful. Clearly the changes which had occurred in the hospital were unsettling to patients and staff, and some painful readjustments were required. The formal structure of the hospital had been changed but the informal organisation of the hospital remained very much out of gear with the new arrangements.

The anxieties provoked by the changes had not been alleviated while the reorganisation was going on and there was little, if any, preparation for the changes. It seemed that the anxiety was expressed in mutual antagonism and particularly in hostility towards individuals who were seen as agents of change. The senior P.S.W. was seen as such an individual by the social workers who found it easier to attack an individual than an impersonal system. The ways in which the social workers perceived the unit system affected their perceptions of the possibilities of co-ordination. They restructured both the implications and the content of the meetings according to their own points of view and sometimes gave communications they received meanings quite different to those which were intended.

The social workers, perhaps as a result of their high level of anxiety about the fluid situation, tended to change their functions in order to try to meet what they perceived their colleagues' expectations to be. Sometimes this led them to quite inappropriate or undesirable behaviour, from a professional point of view. An example is the "dumping" of a patient at a relative's home. Sometimes quite unconsciously, the workers changed or added to their functions converting them to purposes irrelevant or contrary to their original purposes. The tendency to believe that responsibility was so diffused that no one person or group was responsible for a patient provided some defence against anxiety but led to behaviour which might be regarded as irresponsible, and as meeting the needs of the social workers rather than their clients (Day, 1965).

An organisation may attempt to evade anxiety. The idea of a social defence system refers to the institutionalisation of primitive defence mechanisms, comparable to those observed in individuals. The functioning of social defence systems has certain consequences for members of organisations. There may be failure of communication resulting in lack of support for individuals within working relationships. There may be a tendency for psychological distance between workers of different status to be reinforced (Menzies, 1960). Where hierarchical dependence blocks the free flow of communication and thus inhibits the discussion of problems and anxieties, the effectiveness of an organisation in reaching its objectives is hindered. Problem solving and work performance are adversely affected and the dissatisfaction and frustration of members of staff may be shown in a high rate of staff turnover with deterioration in the service available to the organisation's clients. The success and viability of an organisation are intimately connected with the techniques it used to contain anxiety.

One of the problems of large organisations is that they tend to be impersonal in some aspects of administration. Co-ordination of the activities of staff is sometimes awkward, particularly if there is lack of opportunity or ability on the part of individuals or groups to pass on their views to others. When workers are spatially separated they tend to think that their work problems are unique, that they have special priorities and that their claims should take precedence over those of others. The more widely workers are separated spatially and emotionally the more difficult it is for them or anyone else to co-ordinate their work. Where there are personality clashes between work group members together with ignorance of the activities of other workers, problems of co-ordination may be great.

The problem of co-ordination is largely one of communication for without efficient communication no co-ordinated effort is possible. Communication may be defined as the capacity of an individual or group to pass on his feelings and ideas to another individual or group. There are many causes of defective communication. Some of these relate to formal organisation and are defects due to time, space and the divisions of the structure.

All work is related to a time scale. If an individual or group fails to supply another with information at the time they are entitled to expect it, the carrying out of tasks is affected. Spatial distance between workers raises similar problems. The greater the spatial distance between workers in an organisation the greater the difficulty in co-ordinating work. Spatial distance is likely to lead to social distance. When workers have little social contact with one another grievances may develop and there may be deliberate attempts to create problems for other people or to shelve the problems.

A third type of failure in communication arises when work groups fail to co-ordinate their activities for reasons other than space or time factors. Such breaks develop most easily between functionally separate units. Generally speaking it is easier to co-ordinate units doing similar work than those which are performing widely different functions. Conflicts are therefore likely to arise at different levels in a hierarchical organisation. How a person in a middle management position feels and acts depends on whether he is looking down or looking up the structure.

But there are also horizontal divergencies of interest. The basis of this divergence of interests is that each person or unit is under pressure to impress higher management. But the ability to do this depends on co-operation with others at the same level. There is thus a problem of reconciling simultaneous attitudes of competition and co-operation as the history above illustrates.

The desire to please or impress may adversely affect communication by causing information passing up the line to be distorted, so that management is told what people think it wants to hear. Communication down the line may also be distorted. The process of elaboration, making general decisions more specific, may involve errors, delays or omissions. Each person up or down the line acts as an information filter and what arrives at the other end, especially in the case of information passing up the line, may bear very little relationship to the state of affairs as it actually exists (Brown, 1954).

The problems associated with defective communication are closely linked with a weakness of formal organisation, i.e. that it tends to ignore certain emotional factors in human behaviour. It is designed to be rational, logical, and to keep the human factor at a minimum; it is designed to deal with the predictable, the routine and the typical. The irrational and the unforeseen cannot be dealt with easily by formal organisation (Brown, 1954).

The status hierarchy creates obstacles to free communication between members of an organisation. The more unpleasant a position is in a hierarchy the stronger are the forces on a person to transmit messages which are irrelevant to the task in hand. There is a general tendency to restrict messages which would tend to lower one's status position in the eyes of others or which would make one appear incompetent. A hierarchy restrains the communication of criticisms of people at another level but higher status persons feel freer to criticise those of lower status. There is a tendency for low-status people to choose as friends people of high status but high-status people tend to choose others of high status (Kelley, 1951). In another investigation it was found that the individual tends to reduce the psychological distance to the more powerful, and to increase it to less powerful persons. Communication serves as a substitute for upward movement to high-status positions in these instances (Mulder, 1960).

A study of communications in general hospitals noted some apparent effects of hierarchical obstacles to communication (Revans, 1964). The perception which a staff member of medium status, a hospital sister, had of those above her was transmitted to staff who were junior and responsible to her. Several incidents were observed where the junior nurse was unable to approach the sister and the patient was unable easily to approach the junior nurse. It seemed that where the ward sister was not on easy terms with the doctor she could not be on easy terms with her own ward staff. If the doctor appreciated or invited the opinions of the ward sister, she in her turn would be more likely to encourage her nurses to discuss patients with her. This appeared to encourage the nurses to communicate more with the patients.

Discussing the findings, Revans observed that anxiety is a prevalent quality of the hospital. For the doctor, anxiety is increased if he is asked a question by the nurse or patient to which he does not know the answer. A simple way to avoid this threatening situation is to discourage the asking of questions. This leads to uncertainty and increases the level of anxiety; further communication failure may result. The difficulties of

G

communicating and of being communicated with are heightened by unrealistic ideas of one's own role, knowledge and status. The member of staff who discourages questions has an unrealistically defensive image of himself. Such misperception inhibits communication and learning. A vicious circle is thus created. The level of anxiety remains high and further communication failure may result. The role of communication in the co-ordination of social workers' activities will be discussed further in the next chapter.

CHAPTER 7

The Community, the Social Agency and the Social Worker

1. Moral and political issues and communication

Early in the previous chapter I referred to Perlman's view of agencies' functions as reflecting society's will to provide social services. Such a statement of course begs many questions. It assumes, for example, that society (whatever that is taken to mean) agrees about what services to provide, how much of them to provide, and to whom they should be available. Forder (1966) suggests that the community is ambivalent about those who are dependent on it or who fail to live up to generally accepted standards of behaviour. Social services depend on community support for the resources and the powers they need. If it does not give active support the general public at least acquiesces in the spending of their money on social services. The statutory services exist only because the representatives of the community accept their importance and value. But people often also resent the financial demands made by the dependence of others; they complain for example about irresponsible people who "live on the state". They thus have conflicting feelings of concern and intolerance, pity and rejection towards dependent or "deviant" people.

Because of their close acquaintance with areas of unmet need and social injustice it has been recognised that social workers should speak out against bad social conditions and should communicate information about people's needs. But this is not necessarily easy. It is not easy to criticise, or appear to criticise, your employers, for example. Many social workers are reluctant to engage in militant social action. Such action could lead some people to associate the social work profession with the aims and activities of political extremists and it could thus become discredited in the eyes of many citizens. Professional groups may not easily find political allies on the other hand. Barter (1971) has argued that most social workers continue to try to press their clients into a spurious conformity to the wishes of the comfortably off majority of the population. Social workers delude themselves that their efforts to get social deviants to conform to the rules is an expression of love. They ignore the fact that it is a blatant form of social control. But the situation is altering. The new generation of social workers, according to Barter, "rejects the conventional notion of society as a consensus among different groupings. Instead it sees society as a battle between competing interest groups with the game rigged in favour of those who already control more than their fair share of resources".

Social workers have always had to live with dilemmas of multiple choice: helping people to adjust to old or new circumstances; helping to change society or modify the social pressures which contribute to impoverishment or alienation (Younghusband, 1970). Holman (1970) has commented on social workers' potential for bringing about social reform, and specifically on Sinfield's (1969) belief that social workers have a responsibility to create social change. Three objectives appear particularly within the province of social workers: to argue for more resources for the social services; to convince public opinion of the value of social work; to oppose punitiveness in social-service administration. In Holman's view the plight of deprived people is linked to politics and it is hard to see how people committed to reform can stay apart from it.

Holman also quotes Donnison and Chapman's (1965) analysis of the workings of social agencies. The "providers" (mainly social workers) are in a key position because they are in direct contact with the "determiners of demand" (clients) and are able to communicate and interpret expressed need to the "controllers" (committees). In addition, they can try to gain the support of influential persons outside their particular agency. They are thus equipped to create change over the whole of their local authority. In other words, social workers are well placed to initiate new developments. The implications are that social workers would not regard themselves solely as a means of social control, nor as "adjusters" between clients and society, nor as caseworkers, but also as advocates for the socially deprived. Probably social workers have always carried these roles, sometimes emphasising one rather than others, but often trying to carry them in combination. One would not wish to take issue with Holman about this. His stimulating views highlight the question of the role of communication in political action, but before this is discussed I think some problems require attention.

Social problems may be viewed from a number of perspectives. Problems arise in choosing the actions to be made in response. Delinquency and crime can be regarded in a number of ways. Unlawful acts are usually regarded as disturbances of the social order which should be corrected. They may be seen as violations of a moral code; the offender should repent and make amends. We have also learned to see delinquency as sometimes being a cry for help or a form of protest against the social order. Each of these points of view can lead to action partly inconsistent with the others. The definition of social problems becomes more difficult as the relations to be studied and controlled become more complicated and as the values involved vary. Because so many problems involve multiple valuations the means of "treatment" have multi-valued effects. Choice between different courses of action can be influenced by evidence about a social problem—like crime—and about the people involved. Evidence about social situations, however, is not simply analogous to evidence about physical situations. In other words, patterns of social action are not just consistent forms of social behaviour. People's behaviour occurs, at least partly, because of social norms: their ideas of what is the right thing to do. It depends, therefore, on mutual reciprocal expectations as to the likely behaviour of others (Emmet, 1966). The problems involved here are those of distinguishing matters of fact and matters of value and deciding how they influence each other and overlap. We have to distinguish what is (i.e. something for which factual evidence is available) and what ought to be (i.e. a question of evaluation according to moral rules). Using any amount of factual evidence and strictly logical argument it is not possible to *prove* that a certain course of action should, or should not, be chosen. But although moral questions cannot be settled in the same way as factual questions this does not imply moral agnosticism. People assert that one moral belief is more reasonable than another one and say that one person is more unprejudiced or more rational than another in making a moral choice.

It is not always easy to be explicit about the value implications and to trace the likely repercussions of different courses of action. Where there are diverse interests choice is complex. The individuals concerned may not be consciously aware of all their wants; their individual wishes may be mutually inconsistent. They may be unable to see very far ahead to what future commitments present decisions may lead. It is thus difficult to arrive at a collective choice. Value questions tend to be masked beneath instrumental judgements. We are very good at devising means but frequently fail to question the values of actions in themselves. Obviously no instrumental judgement can be final since it has to be assessed by reference to other value judgements. If A is worth doing only because it leads to B, then why is B desirable? Ultimately it has to be decided that something is good in itself.

The discussion so far has interpreted social work actions as forms of moral behaviour (Timms, 1964 b) and as political acts. But it has not analysed the notion of political activity nor the part of communication in this process. According to the dictionary politics is to do with public affairs. Miller (1965) points out that politics is connected with government, or the way things are run. The essence of a political situation as opposed to one of agreement and routine is that someone is trying to do something about which there is disagreement. First and foremost, Miller writes, politics is about policy; policy is a matter of either the desire for change, or the desire to protect something against change. It can be to do with a wish to make the smallest change in a regulation or even in the administration of a regulation just as much as a policy which will affect the fate of a whole country. It is particularly important to recognise that politics is non-moral. Miller explains this by saying that politics can be made to serve as the *means* of carrying through a moral obligation derived from some social situation but does not constitute a moral obligation in itself. Politics is a means of getting things done often with a strong sense of moral urgency but it does not provide this urgency from its own processes. The sense of urgency must come from the social conditions which have generated political action.

All debates about policy imply a belief that human communication has the power to change the values of participants. They assume that communication has a role in defining problems and in evaluating actions to deal with them. The aim of policy-making is to influence events towards more desirable outcomes. It seems to be clear that communication plays a crucial part in political situations. It seems, also, that the demands on communication are rising, and that it is an increasingly complex exercise. It plays a vital part for reasons which are probably fairly obvious. For example, the formulation of policy requires dialogue. Policy has to be explained. This process of explanation is virtually endless since every government is constantly trying to justify its policies, or to generate trust on the part of the electorate. Policy has to be kept under review, but it also has to be implemented. In both of these activities information has to be processed, and the actions that are to be taken have to be discussed, or some attempt has to be made to secure co-operation. The demands on communication are rising in complex societies partly because traditional ways of securing co-operation or compliance often fail in practice. Traditional ways of making people do as they are told are often no longer morally acceptable. I suppose the Oz Trial illustrates this. But there are very effective and sophisticated means available for moulding peoples' attitudes and opinions. Some of these techniques are available to, and are used by, social workers, as I have tried to show earlier. Whoever employs persuasive techniques, it is an open question whether they are properly controlled or properly used. One has to examine individual instances with care and having regard to the range of perspectives that are possible.

2. *Problems of co-operation and co-ordination in social welfare*

We can now go on to consider the crucial position which the social worker often occupies, as information source and advocate, in the community. We may wish to consider whether, in this position, the skills of casework and group-community work are needed. We are back, I think, to the social worker as interpreter and co-ordinator. In view of the complexity of the problems involved, it is hardly surprising that the questions of co-operation between workers in the social services and the co-ordination of social work activities have received a considerable amount of attention (see, for example, H.M.S.O., 1959; Jefferies, 1965; Rodgers and Dixon, 1960; Wedge, 1965). The necessity for improving communication between social agencies, social workers and other people has been influenced by the growing recognition that focusing on only one aspect of the situation of the client and his family does not always lead to the provision of the most adequate service for him. Because of the complexity of many social problems a variety of services is required to develop adequate understanding of the nature of the difficulties and to formulate plans to meet them. This is illustrated by social work undertaken with families with multiple problems. It has been found (Philp, 1963; Wofinden, 1954) that the participation of many community organisations is required if they are to receive effective service. Where help has been given to these families by individual agencies in an unco-ordinated way, often at times of crisis, the help given has been more limited than it would be if effective communication between agencies led to more adequate understanding.

Writing of the situation in the United States, Rice (1960) described communication breakdown between social workers under three main headings: (i) lack of time; (ii) lack of effective agency policy; (iii) resistance. Lack of time is often given as the reason for social workers in a community failing to get together to discuss a problem on which they are all working. But in communities where there has been a well-established method of community case conferences, the required time for such conferences has been found to be far less than the time required for duplicating study of the client's situation. Without communication there is inadequate analysis of the problem and more limited treatment results. Lack of effective policy about communication creates breakdown in co-operation. The policy of restricting the exchange of information, even with qualified social workers in other settings, is still operative in some agencies. This rigid concept of the confidential nature of data obviously limits communication. In accepting the social worker's services the client implicitly trusts the social worker to help him directly and also to help him make use of other services, by sharing information with the staff of these services. In Rice's opinion, all professions have an obligation to exchange information for the purpose of rendering more effective service. Obviously the recipient of such information must be considered capable of using it for the welfare of the client. Under the third heading Rice observed that some social workers are reluctant to share information because of lack of trust in other social workers (particularly the untrained), and in other persons who may be of help to the client. It is essential, in passing on information to another person, that the worker presents it in such a way that it will be clearly understood and properly used.

Stevenson (1963) grouped co-ordination difficulties under four general headings: (a) problems of social philosophy; (b) problems of casework skills; (c) problems of workers' function and involvement; (d) the problems of administrative roles. Suggestions as to why co-ordinating arrangements were only partially successful appeared to be superficial. Stevenson said that a co-ordinating committee consists of people with a diversity of aims and emphasis and the psychological factors which affect such discussions could be discerned. For example, the identifications and personal problems of participants were often clear. Underlying the arguments that a man "ought" to work there might be punishing attitudes not uncommonly found in those whose own sense of duty was harsh. Underlying other arguments there might be sympathy or collusion with the underdog against authority. Pointing this out did not dispose of problems of judgement and decision in weighing up the needs of a family in relation to the needs and rights of others.

At the field-work level there were differences (a) in method and (b) of function and involvement. Friction arose from differences in method and skill and from misunderstandings about different approaches. Difficulties arising from the structure of the social services might be modified by knowledge of the responsibilities of others and by increased emphasis on seeing a family as a whole unit. Such modification could occur as a result of education and training. Stevenson suggested that agency function could reinforce the personal inner identification of the social worker. A kindly mental welfare officer might feel very protective towards a timid and pathetic mother, while an outgoing health visitor who had had to cope with many obstacles in her own life might be intolerant of the mother's hopelessness and feel much more protective towards her children. For different kinds of workers different problems would seem more pressing or more disturbing than others. This added to the tensions in co-ordination. At higher levels in the administrative structure, organisational identifications might have their most serious consequences, an important factor in this being individual's desire for power. At the field-work level organisational identification is instrumental in bringing broad considerations to bear on individual situations. At higher levels identifications serve to predetermine the decision and to introduce among its assumptions unrecognised and unverified valuations. Co-ordination is affected by the extent to which senior officers are able to take a wide view of the responsibilities of their agency in relation to those of others. The senior officer has the task of looking beyond the confines of his own organisation towards the wider values and objectives of the social services as a whole.

More recently Lapping (1971) has suggested that social workers' ability to deal with conflicts with employers or managers and turning them to constructive ends will be a practical measure of how effective they can be. She points out that the nature of their task means that social workers are bound to find themselves in conflict situations. But it is possible for one side or the other to avert destructive flare ups. In her view the greatest responsibility lies with the social workers themselves. She makes the point that activities which involve social workers in the community are more likely to be contentious than the decisions they may take about individual cases. I now discuss some work which appears to be relevant to what Lapping says about the social workers' responsibility. The focus remains on communication as an aspect of effective co-operation.

3. *Facilitating communication: an approach to the co-ordination of social-work services in a county borough*

An article by Harbert (1966) described the writer's experience of responsibility for the co-ordination of social-work services in a county borough. In the authority as a whole the policy adopted by each department tended to split the various social-welfare workers into separate groups with opposing ideas about their functions. Differences also occurred between staff in different sections of the same department and between trained and untrained workers. There was no single pattern of group loyalty throughout the corporation. It seemed evident that people who called themselves social workers or welfare officers could not reach any fundamental agreement about their role in the community. Some adopted a punitive approach to clients who had failed socially and it was difficult for them to see the relevance of confidentiality. This inhibited other workers from contributing during co-ordinating meetings. A good many field workers felt that it was their task to solve all the problems in the families they visited. Others interpreted their duties very narrowly and shut their eyes to everything beyond their own statutory duty. Probably the majority of officers adopted both these attitudes at different times depending on the particular case in hand. When referring a family to another department some staff had unrealistic expectations of what could be achieved. Chief officers were remote from one another and their views about the essence of social work conflicted. It seemed that consequently feelings of rivalry and insecurity were never far from the surface among field staff. The field staff could be conceived as falling into two broad groups. The first group, for convenience, could be referred to as caseworkers—child-care and probation officers, some welfare officers working with the elderly and the physically handicapped, some mental health social workers—who worked with individuals and families to effect change by studying the total problem and providing a therapeutic relationship. The second group, referred to as welfare workers—officers of the National Assistance Board, housing welfare officers, education welfare officers, youth employment officers—were more limited to specific tasks and not primarily concerned with the total care of an individual or family.

At the period described the education welfare service lacked a clearly defined purpose and was failing to attract recruits of the same quality as other services. During regular meetings with staff in different departments it became apparent that education welfare officers saw their role principally as referring agents, passing on the more complex difficulties to specialist workers. They were still known as school attendance officers, they had no recognised training, and their duties were not well defined. Their department could not provide them with the support and guidance they needed. Because of limitations in their basic education it was difficult for them to communicate effectively with younger and more sophisticated officers in other services, and their status was low in their own service. A survey conducted in the authority among council tenants in serious rent arrears (Harbert, 1965) provided striking evidence about the extent to which education welfare officers knew families who were receiving help from other social-work services. One-quarter of the children in these households were being supervised by education welfare officers because of bad school attendance. Almost all of the families were known to other social services. It seemed that it would be wise to devise the best possible means employing education welfare officers. The confusion of thought about social work among elected representatives and senior officers made it difficult to create a climate of opinion in which any group of workers could willingly recognise limitations in their training and abilities, but the senior officers appreciated the need for limitations in the roles of their departments, and that it was impossible for each department to run its own private family service.

It was agreed to arrange meetings between the staffs of a primary and a secondary school and a group of social workers to investigate what kind of problems school teachers had which they would like to bring to the attention of social workers. The meetings threw light on the varying attitudes which participants had towards one another, difficult children and inadequate parents. In the primary school discussion centred round children who came to school in a neglected state and whose parents seemed to lack interest in them. In the secondary school the strongest feelings were directed against unruly boys who could not be disciplined. The teachers were confused by the variety of social agencies all apparently having the same function. They retained a healthy scepticism about the work of these agencies.

At almost every meeting there were occasions when the two groups of workers modified their attitude to a particular family as a result of discussion. The social workers were often surprised to discover that families which they had known for a considerable time were presenting acute problems of a different kind to the school teacher. After approximately six meetings in each school it was clear that an education welfare officer could discover from school staff those families which had serious problems and that they could assist in the supply of information to the appropriate casework organisation. They could visit some families where the situation did not require the use of a caseworker and could report to the appropriate service when necessary.

4. *Communication processes in groups and in the community*

In the Harbert study the members of the groups appear to have shared interests and motivations which led to an opening up of communication, resulting in sharing of information and ideas. The groups seemed to have a feeling of achievement in completing a task, and possibly in planning ahead to work on further problems. The social workers in the psychiatric hospital, described in the previous chapter, were unable to use an opportunity to discuss common problems. The meetings in which they were involved were not perceived in this way, and, unlike the Harbert group, their "leader" was regarded with suspicion and hostility. In fact he was not permitted to "lead" since he could not be accepted as representing the interests of the group. The discussion which follows is about communication in groups, and is focused mainly on collaborative groups. This is because the illustrations given are of groups which were based on this model, even though, of course, the psychiatric hospital group were unable to co-operate to any significant extent. There are other patterns of group organisation, of course, but clear distinctions between authoritative, manipulative, and collaborative groups are difficult to make and somewhat unrealistic. Focusing on the collaborative model does not therefore imply that this is "best" for all purposes. One-way communication is more efficient and speedy than two-way communication, for example, and for some purposes it is more effective.

It is necessary to deal with some topics, very briefly here, as elsewhere in this book. Thus leadership is not fully discussed, and it has not been possible to deal with other important topics. Suggestions about possible useful sources are given later and it is hoped that introducing some of the ideas here will lead you to investigate them more fully elsewhere. Harbert's work shows how learning may occur in a group by allowing

or encouraging members to participate in communication and decision-making. Where individuals can participate reasonably freely in the communication process they are likely to feel committed to further learning. This may be because group participation is a way by which individuals learn social reality.

It cannot, of course, be assumed that a group is receptive and willing to co-operate in discussion or action. We have discussed a resentful and divided group—the social workers in the psychiatric hospital, and other instances where groups were hostile towards outsiders or towards other groups. It is necessary therefore to review some techniques of influence which might be employed in situations where a person and what he wishes to communicate might meet with a hostile or unsympathetic reception. Where an individual is communicating to a hostile group the first problem is to gain their attention. It is probably best to include both sides of the issue, their point of view and the position to which it is desired to convert them. If the message is a negative one people are more likely to accept it if it is preceded by a message which they view favourably. People are more likely to change their opinions if they become emotionally involved before they are given new information. Reversing this order tends to strengthen resistance. If one is seeking (a) to convert a group and at the same time (b) to avoid the dangers of selective listening, it is advisable to initiate communication with a message which is central to the group and with which they can positively identify. Once attention is caught it is possible to turn to less favourable messages. It is necessary to consider the internal structure of the group and to whom a message should be sent. In the hostile group with a hostile leader it might be that messages should be addressed to isolates or to people who are in the process of leaving the group. They may not be as influential as the leader in disseminating the message through the group but they are more likely to attempt to do this than the leader. Deviant members are more open to communications which are hostile to group norms. In the case of the friendly or indifferent group the natural leader is more likely to spread the communicator's message. In order to co-ordinate their efforts people need to know what they may expect from each other. Group members have responsibilities towards their groups; they are responsible for participating in the group and for co-operating with other members in working with them towards its goals. They work with reference to group norms and expectations, both when they are with the group and when they are away from it.

Significant changes in people's behaviour and attitudes occur or can be brought about more quickly if the people who wish to change (or who are expected to change) participate in deciding what the change shall be and how it may be achieved (Batten, 1957). We have already seen that attempts at changing attitudes or behaviour by disseminating information or by rational argument alone are sometimes ineffective or only temporary in their effects. If the people involved in the change participate in making the decision to change they feel more committed to the decision and to acting on it, than if a decision is imposed on them in an authoritative way (Mead, 1958).

The main effect of a collaborative pattern of group organisation or communication is that it is more likely to facilitate interchange of ideas between people. In other words it is more likely to be two-way communication rather than one-way. Two-way communication is likely to be more accurate than one-way communication. This is because people can ask questions and receive answers directly. They can make comments indicating whether or not they have understood a message. Through participation members of a group can help decide how best information may be communicated.

In a two-way communication situation the morale of group members is likely to be higher as a result of participation and emotional involvement. Knowledge of results of their discussions and conversations is also conducive to higher morale. Two-way communication tends to be slower. The possibility of digression and disorderliness is higher than in the one-way communication situation.

The efforts made by individuals must result in satisfaction to the participants as well as helping in the performance of the task. The group leader has to be alert to the needs of members as well as the nature of the task, and it is his function to co-ordinate individual effort. The leader steers or navigates the group so that members are strongly motivated and the purposes of the group are satisfied. His effort is directed towards ensuring that the maximum use is made of the resources of the group. The leader tries to facilitate the work of a group by paying close attention to the verbal and non-verbal communications which pass between the members. He considers, for example, to what extent a question or statement indicates areas of anxiety or uncertainty which appears to hinder the group's work. In the permissive atmosphere of some groups the expression of criticisms, negative attitudes and strong feelings generally is encouraged. Through ventilation of such feelings the group may be able to identify problems of communication as well as problems of task performance. In the long term, as a result, the group may come to perform more effectively. The leader has to assess the extent to which members' contributions help the group in its problem-solving tasks and how they relate to earlier steps towards agreed objectives. He tries to be sensitive to the response which a member may be seeking by differentiating provocative statements which may or may not stimulate further constructive thinking and comments which convey interpersonal hostility or personal frustration. Perhaps a member is seeking reassurance that his contribution is valued. Recognition of this may enable him to develop his contribution in ways which hitherto he has been unable to. In weighing members' demands the leader may influence when or how a demand is met. He has to try to provide a structure for discussion which enables the group to use their time and energy as economically as possible (McCullough and Ely, 1968).

The problems which a group has in clarifying its objectives and the roles of members, including the leader, are obviously complex ones. The problems of the leader in exercising control, through steering the discussion, are also complex. It may be helpful to consider these problems as decisions about what information is relevant and what is irrelevant. In a collaborative group perhaps one of the main barriers to effective communication is superfluous information which has the effect of concealing or distorting the group's aims. In an authoritarian group the problem may be a different one. Communication may be inhibited.

Irrelevant information has previously been described as noise. In the collaborative group, noise will not be eliminated. The leader will try to facilitate its identification. By being brought into the open its effect may be reduced. The group have been involved in formulating their task and are likely to agree broadly about what is relevant information. An authoritarian leader may be able to deal with noise more quickly but repressive action may have after effects in the form of the member who resents having his contribution arbitrarily ruled irrelevant.

Groups are in the community and do not exist in a vacuum. Some groups are in closer contact with other sections of the community than others, of course. Accepting this qualification, processes of communication link various groups in the community, which may be conceived as a network or a system of intergroup relations. The information which flows through the network influences actions in its different parts. The information which is conveyed may be about the attitudes or beliefs of people, or their feelings, or about their proposed actions or actions they have already carried out. In general, individuals are more or less concerned with different aspects of their community. People with similar concerns tend to affiliate with each other and to form groups. In their groups they formulate objectives which reflect their concerns, and groups, using their members, engage in tasks aimed at furthering their aims. People's perceptions of tasks vary and the aims of different groups, like the aims of individuals, are often in conflict. The resolution of intergroup conflict, like the resolution of conflict between individuals, is dependent on a wide range of variables. A basic requirement of a bridging operation, however, is the establishment of effective communication, so that the nature of conflicts can be identified, and in some cases steps can be taken to modify, or hopefully to resolve, some of them.

Notes

Because this book is intended to be an introduction to an important but difficult field of study I have given a full bibliography so that readers wishing to follow up a topic or research area may be able to do this. Secondly, I have documented my sources fully, because it is necessary to draw on different disciplines and I feel it is desirable to show how this attempt has been made. The field of study is wide, however, and no doubt much work of importance has been omitted, or has been referred to only briefly. Because the amount of literature is continually increasing, and also because detailed notes are not given for each chapter, I am adding the following suggestions. They are intended to help readers to save time in following up some subjects and in making good some omissions from the text. They will also provide further indications of the programme of the present book and questions for further work. Most of the books selected here contain detailed references to, or reviews of, other work.

Chapter 1

An interesting introduction to the general topic of communication is the book by Aranguren (1967); Cherry (1961) is also very useful but more difficult: some technical sections should be skipped. Watzlawick *et al.* (1968) is also difficult but repays study, being particularly relevant to the practice of social work. Irvine's article (1955) is a valuable framework for thinking about communication processes in social work. The discussions by Timms (1962 and 1964b) are clear and helpful and they are also useful guides to further sources. Davison (1965) provides a clear account of social casework which serves as a sound basis for further discussion.

Chapter 2

Suggestions for further reading given for Chapter 1 are also relevant to this chapter with the exception of Aranguren. Parry (1967) will be useful in considering the application of certain aspects of psychology in social work. The work of Timms (1962 and 1964b) has already been quoted and should, if necessary, be referred to again by readers of this chapter. This chapter deals mainly with communication between client and social worker. Some readers may find it helpful to read Chapter 6 which deals with the role of communication in making services available. Further reading on this topic which will be helpful in studying the present chapter is Donnison *et al.* (1965). Many students find that Forder (1966) is very helpful in clearing up misunderstanding or confusion. Readers will observe that the topics covered by the umbrella-term communication are studied in many disciplines. For the social worker there are advantages in studies which link different subjects, while recognising that boundaries are ill-defined. Such an approach recognises that the study of social situations is not analogous to study of physical occurrences. Patterns of social inter-action are not just regular forms of behaviour. A person's behaviour occurs at least in part because of social norms. The study of communication processes contributes to our understanding of social expectations. Thus my notes on Chapter 4 make special reference to work on Roles, a promising area of study for social workers and one on which I have relied very much in this book.

Chapter 3

Parry (1967) and Munn (1961) provide some basic theoretical background for this chapter. Abercrombie (1969) is a readable and stimulating reference for per-ception and learning processes. In the notes to Chapter 2 above I referred to people's expectations about their own behaviour and that of other people. When we try to obtain a picture (or series of pictures) of relationships between people we need to recognise that they are each both subject and object. A person responds to others in terms of his own feelings and perceptions and also in terms of what he perceives are the other's responses to him. Laing *et al.* (1966) describes this circular process as the spiral of reciprocal perspectives, as I mentioned in this chapter. This book is recommended for further reading. Argyle (1967) is recommended for basic reading. Cook (1971) has written a review of work on interpersonal perception which should be very useful.

The study of perception in social work is a relatively new area of research, but it would seem to be an important and promising one. Borgatta *et al.* (1960) is not easy reading but should be consulted by the serious student. Meyer and Timms have published a salutary but constructive paper (1969) and for greater detail their book should be consulted. Butrym (1968) made a small study of a medical social work department. As with the other research her working methods should be noted.

Chapter 4

It will be apparent that this book relies greatly on ideas about roles. "Role is potentially a concept of great fertility . . . " writes Ruddock (1969). His book is strongly recommended for further reading and Leonard (1965 and 1966) should also be consulted. Goffman's work discusses general implications of the role concept in a vivid and lively way (Goffman, 1956). The application of these ideas in social work is discussed by Timms (1964) and Perlman (1957 and 1966). The work of Bernstein and the Russian psychologists is succinctly summarised and critically reviewed by Lawton (1968).   Readers interested in the mass media would find Brown (1963) a useful starting p oint. Williams (1968) is also recommended.

Personal construct theory studies persons as interpreters of their environment and themselves. It tries to understand people in terms of the way each "experiences the world" and to interpret their behaviour in terms of what it is designed to signify for the behaving person. A construct, basically, is a discrimination which a person can make (Bannister and Fransella, 1971). This theoretical approach is thus relevant to the work on schemata and cognitive processes discussed in Chapter 3 and in this chapter. It also provides useful psychological insights into the idea of role which it places within the context of someting a person is doing. We try to understand other people in terms of their outlooks. "To the extent that one person construes the construction processes of another he may play a role in a social process, involving the other person" (Kelly, 1966, quoted in Bannister and Fransella, 1971).

Chapter 5

Nursten's article (1965) is a stimulating discussion of the application of Bernstein's hypotheses in social work practice. It should be read in conjunction with this chapter. Jehu (1967) is also relevant. Staats (1968) describes research on some of the topics discussed here. Miller (1951) is a well-established source for work on language. Lyons (1968) is wider in scope and is an advanced textbook. It will be of interest to people wishing to study linguistics in depth. Ogden and Richards (1966) is also advanced and is an established book on problems of meaning. Munn (1961) refers to the semantic differential and a recent article by Jehu (1970) illustrates an interesting use of this method of analysis in social work research. Information about cybernetics is available from Ashby (1968). This is a technical book. Sluckin (1960) is an alternative and has a wider perspective. Two standard social-work textbooks by Hollis (1964) and Perlman (1957) could be read in conjunction with the first five chapters of the present book.

Timms (1969b) opens the third chapter of his book on Child Care with the comment that "the notion of the child as a possible client is a comparatively recent development in casework in this country". He provides helpful illustrations and discussions of considerations arising in casework with children and adolescents in this book. A briefer discussion is to be found in the more general book on Social Casework (Timms, 1964). Casework techniques are discussed in Winnicott's paper (in Younghusband, E. (Ed.), 1966). There are also useful discussions relevant to the topic in Social Work with Families (Younghusband, E. (Ed.), 1965). The papers by Shapiro, Irvine, Lloyd and Woodward in this compilation should be noted. All of these references would interest those wishing to read on communication with the child. Rich (1968) gears his short book to the professional who deals with children. He discusses communication with the "normal" as well as the "disturbed" child. Vann (1971) makes some interesting points in discussing the risk that the needs of the child client might be overlooked.

Chapter 6

Brown, J. (1954), Etzioni (1964) and Blau and Scott (1963) will be useful for further reading. Warham (1967) provides a simpler introduction of direct interest to social workers. Donnison *et al.* (1965) is an important basic source and also leads one's attention towards the next topic in the present book. Eyden (1969) is a valuable complement. In conjunction with these the papers by Parker and Wistrich in Robson, W. and Crick, B. (Eds.) (1970) should be consulted.

It is important to note that in Chapters 6 and 7 ethical and moral considerations cannot be discussed at length. Readers are referred to the social work texts, Timms (1964) being specially useful. Plant (1970) provides a valuable discussion of moral and political aspects of social casework which will be relevant to the next chapter also. The article by Rea Price (1967) is stimulating.

Chapter 7

The literature referred to in the previous chapter is relevant to Chapter 7 also. I think that Forder (1966) (especially Chapter 8 on the Community, Committees, and the Welfare Services and Chapter 10 on Co-operation and Co-ordination) provides a very useful basis for studying the topic. The techniques which have been summarised are discussed at greater length in Leavitt (1964) (Part 4) and Thelen (1967). Psychological studies of persuasive communication are described in Hovland *et al.* (1968). Readers will find it helpful to refer to McCullough and Ely (1968) again and to Batten (1957). Three further publications have to be recommended, namely Holman (1970), Sinfield (1969) and Rein (1970). These should help readers wishing to read on the political implications or context of social work, and to set Chapter 7 in contemporary (1972) perspective.

Bibliography

ABERCROMBIE, M. L. J. (1969) *The Anatomy of Judgement*, Penguin Books.
ACKERMAN, N. (1958) *The Psycho-dynamics of Family Life: Diagnosis and Treatment*, Basic Books, New York.
ALLPORT, G.W. (1963) *Pattern and Growth in Personality*, Holt, Rinehart & Winston.
ARANGUREN, J. L. (1967) *Human Communication*, Weidenfeld & Nicolson.
ARGYLE, M. (1967) *The Psychology of Interpersonal Behaviour*, Penguin Books.
ASHBY, W. R. (1968) *An Introduction to Cybernetics*, Methuen.

BANNISTER, D. and FRANSELLA, F. (1971) *Inquiring Man*, Penguin Books.
BANNISTER, K. *et al.* (1955) *Social Casework in Marital Problems*, Tavistock Publications.
BARTER, J. (1971) A new kind of loving, *The Observer*, 24 October.
BATTEN, T. R. (1957) *Communities and their Development*, Oxford University Press.
BERNE, E. (1966) *Games People Play*, Andre Deutsch.
BERNSTEIN, B. (1958) Some sociological determinants of perception, *British Journal of Sociology*, Vol. 9.
BERNSTEIN, B. (1959) A public language: some sociological implications of linguistic form, *British Journal of Sociology*, Vol. 10.
BERNSTEIN, B. (1961) Social class and linguistic development: a theory of social learning. In HALSEY, A. *et al.* (Eds.) *Education, Economy and Society*, Free Press.
BERNSTEIN, B. (1965) A socio-linguistic approach to social learning. In GOULD, J. (Ed.) *Social Science Survey*, Penguin Books.
BLAU, P. and SCOTT, W. R. (1963) *Formal Organisations*, Routledge.
BORGATTA, E., FANSHEL, D. and MEYER, H. (1960) *Social Workers' Perceptions of Clients*, Russell Sage Foundation (New York).
BOWLBY, J. (1965) *Child Care and the Growth of Love*, Penguin Books.
BROWN, J. A. C. (1954) *The Social Psychology of Industry*, Penguin Books.
BROWN, J. A. C. (1963) *Techniques of Persuasion*, Penguin Books.
BROWN, W. (1960) *Exploration in Management*, Heinemann.
BRUNER, J. S. (1964) The course of cognitive growth, *American Psychologist*, Vol. 19.
BUTRYM, Z. (1968) *Medical Social Work in Action*, G. Bell & Sons.

CHERRY, C. (1961) *On Human Communication*, John Wiley & Sons.
COOK, M. (1971) *Interpersonal Perception*, Penguin Books.

COYLE, G. L. (1965) Concepts relevant to helping the family as a group. In YOUNG-HUSBAND, E. (Ed.) *Social Work with Families*, Allen & Unwin.

DAVISON, E. (1965) *Social Casework*, Bailliere, Tindall & Cox.

DAY, P. R. (1965) Rivalry at work, *Case Conference*, Vol. 12, No. 1.

DAY, P. R. (1968) Communication and social work roles, *Case Conference*, Vol. 15, No. 6.

DIACK, H. (1966) *Language for Teaching*, Chatto & Windus.

DONNISON, D. *et al.* (1965) *Social Policy and Administration*, Allen & Unwin.

DOUGLAS, J. (1964) *The Home and the School*, MacGibbon & Kee.

DREVER, J. (1952) *A Dictionary of Psychology*, Penguin Books.

EMMET, D. (1966) *Rules, Roles and Relations*, Macmillan.

ETZIONI, A. (1964) *Modern Organisations*, Prentice Hall.

EYDEN, J. (1969) *Social Policy in Action*, Routledge.

FORDER, A. (1966) *Social Casework and Administration*, Faber.

GOFFMAN, E. (1956) *The Presentation of Self in Everyday Life*, Edinburgh University Press.

HAMILTON, G. (1946) *Principles of Social Case Recording*, Columbia University Press.

HARBERT, W. (1965) Who owes rent?, *Sociological Review*, Vol. 13, No. 2.

HARBERT, W. (1966) Co-ordination: a beginning, *Case Conference*, Vol. 12, No. 9.

H.M.S.O. (1959) *Report of the Working Party on Social Workers in the Local Authority Health and Welfare Services* (Younghusband Report).

H.M.S.O. (1968) *Report of the Committee on Local Authority and Allied Personal Social Services*, Cmnd. 3703 (Seebohm Report).

HILGARD, E. and BOWER, G. (1966) *Theories of Learning*, Appleton Century, New York.

HOLDER, C. (1969) Temper tantrum extinction: a limited attempt at behaviour modification, *Social Work*, Vol. 26, No. 4.

HOLLIS, F. (1964) *Casework. A Psychosocial Therapy*, Random House, New York.

HOLMAN, R. (1970) Combating social deprivation. In HOLMAN, R. (Ed.) *Socially Deprived Families in Britain*, Bedford Square Press.

HOVLAND, C., JANIS, I. and KELLEY, H. (1968) *Communication and Persuasion*, Yale University Press.

IRVINE, E. (1964) Transference and reality in the casework relationship, *British Journal of Psychiatric Social Work*, Vol. 3, No. 4.

IRVINE, M. (1955) Communication and relationship in social casework, *Social Casework* (U.S.A.), January 1955.

JEFFERIES, M. (1965) *An Anatomy of Social Welfare Services*, Michael Joseph.

JEHU, D. (1967) *Learning Theory and Social Work*, Routledge.

JEHU, D. (1970) The connotative meaning of social work. A semantic differential analysis, *Social Work*, Vol. 27, No. 1.

KATZ, E. and LAZARSFELD, P. (1955) *Personal Influences: The Part Played by People in the Flow of Mass Communication*, Free Press.

KELLEY, H. (1951) Communication in experimentally created hierarchies, *Human Relations*, Vol. 4, No. 1.

LAING, R. D. (1965) *The Divided Self*, Penguin Books.

LAING, R. D., PHILLIPSON, H. and LEE, A. R. (1966) *Interpersonal Perception*, Tavistock Publications.

LAMBRICK, H. (1962) Communication with the patient, *The Almoner*, Vol. 15, No. 7 (Oct. 1962).

LAPPING, A. (1971) Fighting the boss, *The Observer*, 7 November.

LAWTON, D. (1968) *Social Class, Language and Education*, Routledge.

LEAVITT, H. (1964) *Managerial Psychology*, University of Chicago Press.

LEAVITT, H. and MULLER, R. (1951) Some effects of feedback on communication, *Human Relations*, Vol. 4.

LEONARD, P. (1965) Social control, class values and social work practice, *Social Work*, Vol. 22, No. 4.

LEONARD, P. (1966) *Sociology in Social Work*, Routledge.

LEVINE, R. (1965) Treatment in the home. In YOUNGHUSBAND, E. (Ed.) *Social Work with Families*, Allen & Unwin.

LEWIS, M. (1963) *Language, Thought and Personality in Infancy and Childhood*, Harrap.

LURIA, A. and YUDOVITCH, F. (1968) *Speech and the Development of Mental Processes in the Child*, Staples Press.

LYONS, J. (1968) *Introduction to Theoretical Linguistics*, Cambridge University Press.

MAIER, H. W. (1965) *Three Theories of Child Development*, Harper & Row, New York.

MARES, C. (1966) *Communication*, English Universities Press.

MAYER, J. E. and TIMMS, N. (1969) Clash in perspective between worker and client, *Social Casework*, Vol. 50 (Jan. 1969).

MAYER, J. E. and TIMMS, N. (1970) *The Client Speaks*, Routledge.

McCLINTOCK, F. and AVISON, N. (1968) *Crime in England and Wales*, Heinemann.

McCULLOUGH, M. and ELY, P. (1968) *Social Work with Groups*, Routledge.

MEAD, M. (1958) *Cultural Patterns and Technical Change*, Mentor Books.

MENZIES, I. (1960) A case study in the functioning of social systems as a defence against anxiety, *Human Relations*, Vol. 13, No. 2.

MEYER, C. H. (1970) *Social Work Practice*, Free Press.

MILLER, J. (1965) *The Nature of Politics*, Penguin Books.

MULDER, M. (1960) The power variable in communication experiments, *Human Relations*, Vol. 13, No. 3.

MUNN, N. (1961) *Psychology*, Harrap.

NEWMAN, A. D. (1966) Constructing a pattern of thinking. In Association of Social Workers: *New Thinking About Administration*.

NEWSON, J. and E. (1968) *Four Years Old in an Urban Community*. Allen & Unwin.

NURSTEN, J. (1965) Social work, social class and speech systems, *Social Work*, Vol. 22, No. 4.

OGDEN, C. and RICHARDS, I. (1966) *The Meaning of Meaning*, Routledge.

PARKER, R. (1970) The future of the personal social services. In ROBSON, W. and CRICK. B. (Eds.) *The Future of the Social Services*, Penguin Books.

PARRY, J. (1967) *The Psychology of Human Communication*, University of London Press.

PARSLOE, P. (1967) *The Work of the Probation and After Care Officer*, Routledge.

PARSONS, T. and BALES, R. (1955) *Family Socialisation and Interaction Process*, Free Press.

PERLMAN, H. (1957) *Social Casework*, University of Chicago Press.

PERLMAN, H. (1966) The role concept and social casework. In YOUNGHUSBAND, E. (Ed.) *New Developments in Casework*, Allen & Unwin.

PHILP, A. F. (1963) *Family Failure*, Faber.

PIAGET, J. (1952) *The Origins of Intelligence in Children*, International University Press, New York.

PICARDIE, M. (1967) Learning theory and casework, *Social Work*, Vol. 24, No. 1.

PLANT, R. (1970) *Social and Moral Theory in Casework*, Routledge.

POLLAK, O. (1960) A family diagnosis model, *Social Service Review*, Vol. 34, No. 1.

REA PRICE, J. (1967) The social pathology: a dilemma for social work, *Case Conference*, Vol. 13, No. 12.

REIN, M. (1970) The cross roads for social work, *Social Work*, Vol. 27, No. 4.

REVANS, R. (1964) The morale and effectiveness of general hospitals. In MC-CLACHLAN, G. (Ed.), *Problems and Progress in Medical Care*. Oxford.

RICE, E. (1960) Inter agency communication, *Social Casework*, Vol. 41, No. 5.

RICH, J. (1968) *Interviewing Children and Adolescents*, Macmillan.

ROBSON, W. and CRICK, B. (Eds.) (1970) *The Future of the Social Services*, Penguin Books.

RODGERS, B. and DIXON, J. (1960) *Portrait of Social Work*, Oxford University Press.

RUDDOCK, R. (1969) *Roles and Relationships*, Routledge.

SAPIR, E. (1921) *Language*, Harcourt, Brace & World Inc.

SCHERZ, F. (1963) Family interaction: some problems and implications for casework. In PARAD, H. and MILLER, R. (Eds.) *Ego, Oriented Casework*, Family Service Association of America.

SIMON, H. (1965) *Administrative Behaviour*, Free Press.

SINFIELD, A. (1969) *Which Way for Social Work?* Fabian Society.

SLUCKIN, W. (1960) *Minds and Machines*, Penguin Books.

SPIEGEL, J. (1961) The resolution of role conflict within the family. In BELL, N. and VOGEL, E. (Eds.) *A Modern Introduction to the Family*, Routledge.

STAATS, A. W. (1968) *Learning, Language and Cognition*, Holt, Rinehart & Winston.

STARK, F. B. (1959) Some barriers to client worker communication at intake, *Social Casework*, April 1959.

STEVENSON, O. Co-ordination reviewed, *Case Conference*, Vol. 9, No. 8.

THELEN, H. (1967) *Dynamics of Groups at Work*, University of Chicago Press.

THOMAS, E. *et al.* (1955) The expected behaviour of a potentially helpful person, *Human Relations*, Vol. 8, No. 2.

TIMMS, N. (1962) Communication and collaboration, *The Almoner*, Vol. 15, No. 7.

TIMMS, N. (1964a) The role of the social worker, *New Society*, 3 September.

TIMMS, N. (1964b) *Social Casework*, Routledge.

TIMMS, N. (1969a) *Rootless in the City*, National Council for Social Service.

TIMMS, N. (1969b) *Casework in the Child Care Service*, Butterworths.

VANN, J. (1971) The child as a client of the Social Services Department, *British Journal of Social Work*, Vol. 1, No. 2.

VYGOTSKY, L. (1962) *Thought and Language*, M.I.T. Press, Cambridge, Mass.

WARHAM, J. (1967) *An Introduction to Administration for Social Workers*, Routledge.

WATZLAWICK, P. *et al.* (1968) *Pragmatics of Human Communication*, Faber.

WEAKLAND, J. (1960) The "double-bind" hypothesis of schizophrenia and three party interaction. In JACKSON, D. (Ed.) *The Etiology of Schizophrenia*, Basic Books, New York.

WEDGE, P. (1965) *Preston Family Welfare Survey*, County Borough of Preston.

WHORF, B. L. (1956) Science and linguistics. In CARROLL, J. (Ed.) *Language Thought and Reality*, Wiley, New York.

WILLIAMS, R. (1968) *Communications*, Penguin Books.

WINNICOTT, C. (1966) Casework techniques in the child care service. In YOUNG-HUSBAND, E. (Ed.) *New Developments in Casework*, Allen & Unwin.

WOFINDEN, R. (1954) A note on multiplicity of home visiting by medico-social workers, *Medical Officer*, Vol. 91, No. 83.

YOUNGHUSBAND, E. (Ed.) (1965) *Social Work with Families*, Allen & Unwin.

YOUNGHUSBAND, E. (1970) Social work and social values, *Social Work Today*, Vol. 1, No. 6.

Index

ABERCROMBIE, M. 40, 111
Abstract thinking 40
ACKERMAN, N. 50
Adaptation 68, 73
Adult offenders 79
Advice 17
Advocate 92
Agency function 92, 97
Agents of change 92
Alienation from society 1
ALLPORT, G. 25, 38
Ambiguous communication 48
Angular transactions 45
Anxiety 20, 41, 54, 86–90
ARANGUREN, J. 4, 111
ARGYLE, M. 108, 111
ASHBY, W. 109, 111
Attitudes 18, 25, 50, 54, 103, 104
Authority 39, 52, 54, 55, 61, 65, 75

BANNISTER, D. and FRANSELLA, F. 109
BANNISTER, K. 46
Barriers to communication 35–37
BARTER, J. 92
BATTEN, T. 103, 111
Behaviour change 22, 25, 43, 78, 103
BERNE, E. 45
BERNSTEIN, B. 53, 111
Blaming the environment 52
BLAU, P. and SCOTT, W. 110, 111
BORGATTA, E. 108
BOWLBY, J. 73
BROWN, J. 27, 80, 110, 111

BRUNER, J. 71
BUTRYM, Z. 108, 111
BROWN, W. 81

Change 20, 25, 26, 102
Channels of communication 23, 28
CHERRY, C. 4, 5, 6, 107
Child 109
Childrens' insecurity 47
Client 17
Clues 48
Coding 8–9
Coercion 43, 54
Cognition 8, 25, 39, 40
Collaborative groups 103
Combinations of media 23
Communication of evidence 84
Communication problems 35
    multiple causation 87
    factors in 54
    and time and space 87
Competition 84
Complementary roles 44
Complementary transactions 45
Concept formation 8
Conceptualisation 72
Concrete operations 69
Condensation 12
Conditioned reflex 69
Conditioning processes 72
Confidentiality 96
Conflict 2, 46, 91
Conformity 43, 91

117

Context 10, 12, 38
Contradiction 48
Control 2
Conversation 12
COOK, M. 108
Cooperation and coordination 95–98
Coping 22, 68
Courteous reception 18
COYLE, G. 50
Crisis 68
Critical size of group 79
Criticism 84
Crossed transactions 45
Cultural deprivation 73
Cultural norms 50
Culture 50
Cybernetics 6

DAVISON, E. 14
DAY, P. 84, 87
Deaf children 72
Decision making 103
Defence mechanism 41ff
Deficient language development 73
Delinquency 50
Development, intellectual and linguistic 71
Developmental processes 69
DIACK, H. 11
Distortion of messages 48
Doctors' attitudes 89
DONNISON, D. 78, 92, 110
Double bind 48
DOUGLAS, J. 52
Dreams 12
DREVER, J. 39
Duplex transactions 45

Ego-states 45
Elaborated code 53
EMMET, D. 93

Emotional factors 8, 40
Emotional support 20
Enacted role 45
Environment 1, 72–74
Equilibrium 13
ETZIONI, A. 110
Expressive behaviour 24
EYDEN, J. 110

Face-to-face communication 79
Failure of communication 57, 88
Family 48
Family tasks 51
Family Discussion Bureau 46
Feedback 13
Financial help 18
First signal system 69
Force 43
FORDER, A. 91, 110
Freud 12
Friendly relations in organisations 82
Frustration 52, 88

Gesture 22
GOFFMAN, E. 39, 109
Group norms 43, 102
Guilt 41, 54

Halo effect 38
HAMILTON, G. 83
HARBERT, W. 100
Hierarchy 89
HILGARD, E. and BOWER, G. 69
HOLDER, C. 74
HOLLIS, F. 109
HOLMAN, R. 92
Home visit 68
Hostile group 102
Hostility 84
HOWLAND, C. 110

Iconic representation 71
Ideas and messages 11
Identification 42
Ignorance of role requirements 44
Imagination 70
Inappropriate behaviour 48
Incentive 84
Incongruence 47
Information 4, 18, 43
Information theory 5
Injunction 47
Injustice 91
Institutionalisation 73
Intake interviews 36
Intelligence tests (verbal) 73
Interaction 5
Interdependence of roles 42
Interpersonal perception 31, 37
Interpretation 12–14, 41
IRVINE, E. 54
IRVINE, M. 107

JEFFERIES, M. 95
JEHU, D. 74, 109
Junior staff and ward sisters' attitudes
    89

Knowledge and action 27
Knowledge of social services 37

LAING, R. 42, 108
LAMBRICK, H. 23
Language 8, 53, 68
LAPPING, A. 98
LAWTON, D. 53, 109
Leadership 101
Learning 14, 90, 108
LEAVITT, H. 110
    and MULLER, R. 13
LEONARD, P. 43, 108

Letters 83
Levels of communication 47
LEWIS, M. 73
Listening 28, 76
Local Authority Social Services Act 1970
    78
LURIA, A. and YUDOVITCH, F. 71
LYONS, J. 109

MAIER, H. 7
MARES, C. 8
Marital problems 46
Mass media 50
Material help 18, 65
McCLINTOCK F. and AVISON, N. 1
McCULLOUGH, M. and ELY, P. 104
MEAD, M. 103
Meaning 5, 10
Media 10
Meetings between social workers and
    teachers 100
MENZIES, I. 87
Message 8
MEYER, C. H. 1
MEYER, J. and TIMMS, N. 108
Middle-class parents 54
MILLER, G. 109
MILLER, J. 94
Moral beliefs 93
Motivation 41
MULDER, M. 89
Multiple choice dilemmas 92
MUNN, N. 108

Networks 6, 21, 28
Neurotic needs 46
NEWMAN, A. 80
NEWSON, J. and E. 52
Noise 8
Non-verbal communication 22
NURSTEN, J. 59–60, 109

Objectives of social agencies   79
Observation   28
OGDEN, C. and RICHARDS, I.   109
Opinions   103
Orectic representation   70
Organisation
   efficiency   77, 84
   formal   86
   goals   79
   tasks   77, 80
Organisation of thought   27

Parent–child relationship   65
Parents' values   49
PARKER, R.   110
PARRY, J.   26, 108
PARSLOE, P.   79
PARSONS, T. and BALES, R.   49
PAVLOV, I.   69
Perception   8, 26, 39, 51, 56
Perceptual defence   48
PERLMAN, H.   51, 78, 91, 109
Personal construct theory   109
Personal contact and attitude change   26
Persuasion   43, 50, 110
Phantasies   46
PHILP, A. F.   96
PIAGET, J.   70
PICARDIE, M.   74
Planned behaviour   72
PLANT, R.   110
Politics   94
POLLAK, O.   50
Position   44
Power   78
Pragmatics   5
Prescribed role   44
Primary group   43, 79
Probation and After-care officer   79
Problem solving   13
Projection   41
Propaganda   3

Psychiatric hospital   84
Psycho-analytic ideas   41, 46
Psychological distance   89
Psychological set   8
Public relations   18
Punishment of children   54

Qualifying what is said   48
Questioning   18
Questions, discouragement of   90

Rapport   27
Rationalisation   41
Receiver   41, 102
Reception   9
Reciprocal perspectives   42
Records   82
Redundancy   12
Reference group   43
Referrals to social workers   17
Regression   41
Regulation of behaviour   72
REIN, M.   110
Reinforcement   72
Relationship   14, 45, 54
Relationships between data   48, 69, 70
Remembering   70
Rent arrears   100
Report of the Working Party on Social
   Workers in Local Authority Health
   and Welfare Services: H.M.S.O.
   1959   95
Repression   41
Resistance   36
Resources   1, 77
Restricted code   53
REVANS, R.   89
RICE, E.   96
RICH, J.   110
RODGERS, B. and DIXON, J.   96
Role   38, 42, 44–45, 51, 56, 57, 95, 97,
   104, 108
RUDDOCK, R.   108

Schema 39
Scherz, F. 50
Schizophrenia 48
Second signal system 69
Self-awareness 5, 72
Self-consciousness 4
Self-control 64
Self-esteem 39, 75
Self-image 39
Semantics 4
Semantic differential 109
Sensori-motor stage 69
Set 8
Sign 7, 9
Signal 9, 69
Simon, H. 82
Simple transactions 45
Sinfield, A. 92, 110
Sluckin, W. 109
Social action 91
Social adaptation 73
Social agency 17, 43, 79, 91, 97
Social casework 14
Social class and communication 53
Social control 43
Social defence system 87
Social differences and language use 53
Social distance 87
Social institutions 53
Socialisation 49
Social maladjustment 73
Social norms 43, 53, 102
Social services departments 78
Social welfare 78
Social work practice 55
Society 78, 91
Staats, A. 109
Status 23, 89
Stereotyped responses 37
Stevenson, O. 97
Stimulus 4, 38
Stress 14
Structuring 5, 38

Styles of communication 56
Subjective role 45
Support 20
Symbols 10, 70
Syntactics 4
Systems 10

Television violence and delinquency 50
Tension 14, 26
Thelen, H. 110
Thinking 13, 70
Timms, N. 2, 21, 79, 94, 107, 109
Transmission 4, 10
Trial and error 13
Trust 97ff
Types of speech system 56

Ulterior transactions 45
Unconscious 41
Unconscious collusion 46
Unconscious needs and provoking behaviour 46
Unpleasant position in hierarchy 89
Urban life and social problems 1

Values 94
Vann, J. 109
Vygotsky, L. 71

Warham, J. 82, 110
Watzlawick, P. 6, 107
Weakland, J. 48
Wedge, P. 96
Williams, R. 2, 5, 115
Winnicott, C. 115
Wistrich, E. 110
Withdrawal from society 1
Wofinden, R. 115
Words and gestures 22
Working-class parents 54

Younghusband, E. 92